Inexhaustible

Grace

God's Strength Alive in You

Bishop Demetrius J. Sinegal

Inexhaustible Grace

Copyright © 2017 for The Prophets House Publishing Company

Follow Bishop Sinegal on instagram @Bishop Sinegal and on Facebook book @Bishop Demetrius J. Sinegal.

Dedication

I dedicate this to the body of Christ. It is my desire that through the bit of revelation God has given me concerning grace you might find strength in your times of weakness.

To my wife. You are a shining example of a woman under grace. Denying the government of the flesh and its nature in order to walk out and carry out God's will in the earth! I'm proud of the woman you are and the great woman of God you have become. I love you more than I can express.

Table of Contents

Introduction

I believe that grace is one of the most perverted subject matters of our present age of the church, not because grace is perverted but because its application has been changed from its original intent and original purpose.

Grace was never designed to be a license to sin. It is freedom from sin. It is one of the most powerful gifts of God and if received properly it will radically change your life.

As you read this book please read it with an open mind and heart. My desire is to see you live a life of strength and peace and true holiness. Holiness has nothing to do with surface-level behavior modifications. Holiness is your position in God. You are set aside for him.

Chapter One

Transposed Grace

For there are certain men crept in unawares, who were before of old ordained to this condemnation, ungodly men, turning the grace of our God into lasciviousness, and denying the only Lord God, and our Lord Jesus Christ.

. *Jude 1:4*

My first official role in ministry was as a musician. As a small child my family attended a small church in Gulfport, Mississippi, "First United Gospel Assembly". It was there that an interest began to pique for playing the keyboard.

The Lord had anointed my ear for music. If I could hear it I could play it ... well, at least some simplified elementary version of it. But I could find the key and find the melody. Although I could perhaps find the key and play the melody, I was not well versed in every key. My comfort zones were E flat, and B flat. Then it

7

happened! I discovered I really could play in every key while remaining in the familiar keys of my comfort zones (E flat and B flat) with the simple touch of a button.

Without the discipline, practice, or commitment to learning I had a way to bypass time and still arrive at my end goal of playing in every key. Without any minute investment in the affective domain (a willingness to receive, internalize, and share what is learned), the cognitive domain (the expanding and acquiring of knowledge), or at least the psychomotor domain (actually developing the skill) I still reached my end goal. Never mind that in doing so I had in particular and significant ways completely disregarded any true sense of musical appreciation and adaptation, but none of this came to mind. My sole focus was that I'd reached my end goal.

After all, didn't bypassing time and not having to be taught give me bragging rights? "I'm self-taught," "I "play by ear," "If I can hear it I can play it." All of these things were true; however the depth of that truth was intrinsically connected to the power of the transpose button. If we were to examine the etiology of skill and the development thereof wouldn't we find that time, development, perhaps even mentorship were essential factors in possessing true skill beyond its raw state? I'd bypassed musical theory, had no real command of modes (though I'd later get this), and for being a kid musician that button gave me the advantage that time and experience had not yet afforded me.

I then practiced transitioning between the keys using the transpose button so it was seamless. So to the ear it sounded as though I was smoothly moving through the various keys like a pro. I invested the time to learn the short cut but not to learn the skill. How often is this the truth of the average? Consider a skilled thief. They invest the time to case the place they intend to rob and to learn the security protocols but not to use that same brain power and attention to detail to obtain gainful employment. While you read that paragraph perhaps you shook your head in agreement, but we rarely realize how deeply this kind of laziness and disregard for due process is embedded in our various cultures.

The land of microwaves is where most of us live. We want everything quick, fast and in a hurry without having to learn a recipe, control the temperatures, or stir the pots to ensure nothing burns. Pop it in the microwave, press a couple of buttons and a few minutes later, presto! But the reality is that microwave-cooked food will never taste like a fresh home-cooked meal. You've been to a restaurant before where your food came out cold, right? Even worse, a restaurant that you frequent and a meal that you frequent. After calling over your waiter and informing them, they tell you they're going to have it remade for you. A few minutes later, a piping-hot plate comes out and you say, "That was quick." After tasting the food you can obviously tell that this is not new food but that it is the same plate that has been microwaved.

You're able to taste the difference immediately. The plate looks neat, was presented as though it's new and fresh, but it's simply not the same. It has bypassed the process. The absence of the time spent over the flame, the type of flavor that only comes from the disciplined experience of a well-trained chef is obvious to the discerning palate. The deciding factor in whether or not you keep the plate is not how hungry you are but how hungry you are for a fresh plate of food. If you just want to eat, you'll keep the plate of

food. But if getting a fresh, well-balanced, proper meal is important you'll wait until it's done right. In our culture and in our time fresh, well-balanced and proper take a back seat to quick, fast, and in a hurry, not only in the kitchen, and at the dinner table, but in our spiritual lives. The strength of the word has become less and less important. People join churches for its programs and leave churches for lesser reasons, such as offense and disappointment of not getting a position they desired.

In the day that the outpouring of the Holy Spirit, the presence of God, and a sure word were most important, the length of services was not a major concern. In this day, the 90-minute service, 25-minute sermon, and five-minute altar call are some of the main draws to an "environment of faith". Once we pursued men and women of faith based on the purity of their word; the potency of the power in their word to find the error in your life and draw you towards righteousness and their own capacity to commit to striving towards perfection were non-negotiable. Today, there's been a major transition in environments of faith. Now people are drawn to messages that endeavor to be sensitive so as not to step on any toes. They are drawn to the "inspirational and motivational" message rather than the message of strength, the call to step up to the fullness of who God has purposed them to be. No longer does the exposure of unrepentant immorality and sin guarantee that a faith leader will be sat down or rebuked. Now such an exposure in some cases draws the people towards that person. Not for restoration, definitely not for correction, but to actually partner and follow them. Why? Because they've found common ground and comfort. One's own indiscretions find comfort in an environment where indiscretions are not problematic. Why should you have to live a life of discipline if the leader lives frivolously, failing to consider the writing of Paul the Apostle, in *1 Corinthians 8:9 "But take heed lest by any means this liberty of yours become a stumbling block to them that are weak."*

Not only has this vacating of a life of commitment to discipline become a stumbling block, it has also become a snare, grabbing as many people as it can into its teeth. Now what once convicted them no longer does. They've dismissed the conviction and demonized it calling it condemnation and have created an appetite to take comfort in the things that were once less than desirable for one who professed faith in Christ Jesus to be found bound to. Godly character is the result of a life of forced discipline. However, the new name for what we would have once called acceptance of sin, ungodliness, and the weakness of the flesh is now grace. Grace has been made the covering for sin and that is not at all what grace is. Grace does not give you a license to sin. Grace gives you a license to live through Christ and **NOT** sin.

The true message of grace is not license to sin or to quit. It's not encouragement to be weak or to give up. That would diminish the entire message of the Kingdom, the message that Jesus came preaching. The message of the Kingdom is one of STRENGTH, purporting and encouraging hostile takeovers. The first place this hostile takeover must take place is between the born-again spirit and the unregenerated flesh. Jude urges us in 1:3–4 to

contend and defend this faith that was once delivered to us. *"Beloved, when I gave all diligence to write unto you of the common salvation, it was needful for me to write unto you, and exhort you that ye should earnestly contend for the faith which was once delivered unto the saints. For there are certain men crept in unawares, who were before of old ordained to this condemnation, ungodly men, turning the grace of our God into lasciviousness, and denying the only Lord God, and our Lord Jesus Christ."*

The real message of true grace is not permission to sin or that you're covered to sin. That's a false gospel. That's not good news! "Hey, you can be weak if you want to be, you're covered!" What's so good about that? The true message of grace is that you are free from sin through Christ. You are not freed to it. The liberty is FROM it! You are free FROM the curse of sin and death. Now that is good news! Jude is concerned that the gospel, the good news, has been removed. What is the gospel? It is what I previously mentioned. It is The Kingdom of God and the name of Jesus Christ that the believers heard Phillip preach in Acts 8:12. The Kingdom is the King's dominion. It is the news that His dominion has been given to you and that only through you can He continue to move, tear down, and set up in the earth. The Kingdom is the message of strength that is the original cultural commission of Genesis 1:28; to have dominion, THAT has been restored to you. Now does that sound like a message of acceptance of weakness, defeat, or low-level living? No! However, without making the life of

Jesus and His disciples the source and standard for assessing the ontological, epistemological, and axiological propositions that have been advanced surrounding grace, we will be deceived into thinking that grace is some blanket that loosely covers us.

Some of the most noted pulpiteers that have taken to preaching (what I call) "cheap grace" have gone as far as to say because of grace repentance is not necessary. In its most extreme form a greater heresy has come to the surface in the "gospel" of inclusion; the heretical teaching that none will experience the fires of hell because all have been redeemed by the power of the grace of Jesus Christ (universal reconciliation). In my view, a lack of understanding of the true meaning of grace has contributed to the manipulating of its purpose and power. If asked, the average believer would say that the definition of grace is "God's unmerited favor." If you were in need of a bill being paid and I gave you the money to pay the bill that money would represent my act of kindness. But the money in and of itself is not kindness. In like manner, though grace is an act of unmerited favor, it is not unmerited favor.

Hyper-dispensationalists take some of the Pauline writings to support their error. We'll discuss this a bit later. However the definition of grace is not "God's unmerited favor." Grace is NOT "unmerited favor" of unmerited favor. The word "grace" is from the Greek word

> **Charis -** *the spiritual condition of one governed by the power of divine grace.*

To sum it up, grace is **divine enablement**. It is the strength of Christ working on and within you. It is Christ working through you. It is not you working, it is not you trying, it is not you striving, nor is it you giving

19

in. It is Him at work through you. To suggest that the freedom to fall in sin is the work of grace diminishes the strength of Christ and the work of the cross. To say that grace is the cover-up for your sin, to make it the "get out of jail free card" is again to diminish the power of Christ. God made flesh who was so disciplined in his fleshly incarnation that He could restrain Himself from summonsing angels to defend him. He lived such a life of forced discipline that rather than pronouncing a curse upon those who were being used to execute His death sentence, He prayed "Father, forgive them for they know not what they do." Christ had such control over His body that He chose to deny the pangs of hunger for 40 days while in fasting and prayer; yet this cheap grace says that when you throw yourself upon the grace of Christ you don't have to worry about having to deny your flesh. How great of a juxtaposition.

According to 1 Corinthians 1:4 it is only through grace

that we receive grace. *" I always thank my God for*

you because of his grace given you in Christ

Jesus." So though His example was one of great

discipline and restraint we've somehow slipped into

doing what we want, doing what makes us happy, no

matter how greatly it might oppose the true values of

holiness and Christianity.

> *1 Corinthians 15:9–10 For I am the least of*
> *the apostles and do not even deserve to be*
> *called an apostle, because I persecuted the*
> *church of God. 10 But by the grace of God I*
> *am what I am, and his grace to me was not*
> *without effect. No, I worked harder than all*
> *of them—yet not I, but the grace of God that*
> *was with me.*

Even Paul acknowledged how the grace of God

works. It was not without effect. It gives you strength

to work harder than ever before. True grace has a

strengthening effect in the life of those walking in grace. But more than just you working, it is Christ at work through you. Grace is the END of you and the beginning of Christ in you. If it's the beginning of Christ in you it's the END of all struggles in you because it is no longer YOU that lives.

> *Galatians 2:16–21 "know that a person is not justified by the works of the law, but by faith in Jesus Christ. So we, too, have put our faith in Christ Jesus that we may be justified by faith in[a] Christ and not by the works of the law, because by the works of the law no one will be justified. 17 "But if, in seeking to be justified in Christ, we Jews find ourselves also among the sinners, doesn't that mean that Christ promotes sin? Absolutely not! 18 If I rebuild what I destroyed, then I really would be a lawbreaker. 19 "For through the law I died to the law so that I might live for God. 20 I have been crucified with Christ and I no*

longer live, but Christ lives in me. The life I now live in the body, I live by faith in the Son of God, who loved me and gave himself for me. 21 I do not set aside the grace of God, for if righteousness could be gained through the law, Christ died for nothing!"

Grace through Christ is the end of your struggles. This is why you no longer have to be bound to sin. He's already conquered it, and through Him YOU too can conquer it. Now that's gospel! That's good news. When you try to do it on your own merit, when you lie down in the very sin He died to free you from, you make the Cross of none effect.

So Jude is concerned that the gospel (message of dominion/strength) has been removed. We see the gospel at work in Paul's life in 1 Corinthians 9:27 where he said, *"No, I strike a blow to my body and make it my slave so that after I have preached to others, I myself will not be disqualified for the prize."* Paul said he took dominion over his body. He didn't allow the weakness of the flesh to control him and subsequently disqualify him. Jude is concerned that the gospel has been removed.

He said FIGHT FOR IT because some have turned grace into LEWDNESS. The word "turned" (Jude 1:4) is the Greek word "metatithemi". It means to transpose. Thayer, the Greek scholar that many of our Greek study Bibles and commentaries are built upon, gave us this understanding and definition. It does not mean to "transform". It means to TRANSPOSE; to go up in the key while staying in the same place on the keyboard. The work, the discipline, and the commitment have been bypassed and omitted. The original key (grace) has been transposed into ANOTHER THING. He said it was once and for all delivered to us. This gospel, the Kingdom, His dominion, His strength, the closing of the gap between God and man, it has been delivered to us. Why go back to living a life governed by a weak flesh?

Jude notes this new/false gospel has been forced subtly upon us. How so? Our favorite preacher is now preaching it. The books on the *New York Times* bestsellers lists are talking about it. It sounds so loving, and gentle, and kind, wooing us to sleep, all the while never becoming conscious of the change that has been taking place. It comes in subtly yet systematically. Vs. 11 says first "they go the way of Cain." What does that mean? You remember Cain. He was upset that his offering was rejected. He thought he could give God just anything. He thought that his own efforts were of principal importance and God would have to accept that he was "doing his best". Then it progresses in the text to "the way of Balaam".

Remember in Numbers 22–23, he was a prophet for hire. His gifts were solely for sordid gain. He was a spiritual prostitute. We see this happening today. The attitude of "just receive what I'm giving" followed by the most gifted of us foregoing commitment, loyalty, and covenant in order to be bought by the highest bidder. Musicians that will leave the small church who gave them a chance and a check when no one else would the minute the mega church offers them $1k a week; the pastor who will cancel his commitment to be at one place because another place with more prestige and influence has opened up. People who will quit a covenant relationship, be it marriage or church partnership, in order to pursue what is most convenient.

It doesn't stop there there. The next turn (vs. 11) is the way of Korah. Korah was the elder who led the mass rebellion against Moses. Rebellion is evidence of having left grace. It's not evidence of walking in it. It is the evidence of bondage to the government of the flesh. It is not the evidence of spiritual freedom. He's saying when grace is removed, licentiousness rules. When grace is removed, sin takes over. When grace is removed, your word no longer matters. You dismiss your vows and commitments without a second thought. You'll leave where you've been without feeling you owe an explanation.

You'll return to your old ways and old self in the name of being free when in reality it is a return to the bondage of sin. Why be bound in the name of liberty? That's an oxymoron. Be FREE from the control of the flesh not free to yield to the flesh. Come to the end of yourself and to the beginning of Him. Walking in grace takes the pressure off of you.

Matthew 11:28 "Come to me, all you who are weary and burdened, and I will give you rest. 29 Take my yoke upon you and learn from me, for I am gentle and humble in heart, and you will find rest for your souls. 30 For my yoke is easy and my burden is light."

That's what grace is supposed to feel like. It should be LIGHT! If we could sum it up into one word, walking in grace is being at **rest.** It's the sense of euphoria, comfort, and security that David talks about in Psalms 23. Verse 2 says, *"he leads me beside still waters, he restores my soul..."* He can't lead you if you are being led by your flesh, your feelings, your sins, your emotions. In order to be led you have to be at rest and totally dependent on the one leading you. When grace is transposed to lasciviousness, it makes life hard. In the latter part of Proverbs 13:15 it says, "the way of the transgressor is hard." The word "transgressor" in the Hebrew is the word "bagad". It means the faithless or the unfaithful. When the children of Israel came out of Egypt, they cried for the food of Egypt, savory things that had to be picked up off of the ground. In order to pick these vegetables you've got to be bent over. Have you ever done a job that requires you to bend your back all day? It's painful! However, the fruit of the Promised Land is MILK AND HONEY, grapes, and sweet fruit. That's easy picking. It is not God's desire for you to toil all night and catch nothing. The power of Grace is the power to be at rest.

Now, the Promised Land of today is not a geographical place, it's a REST PLACE. It's a place your spirit man comes to where it is unmoved, it's not anxious, and it's definitely not at odds with the righteousness of Christ. It's where you've accepted

29

His righteousness upon you. You're no longer fighting with the lust of the flesh or the pride of life. You choose to yield to His grace and allow it to work on your behalf. It is the place where you are totally and completely dependent on His work. That, my friends, is the work of grace.

Chapter Two

Cursed No More

Admittedly, I took a moment to give God praise after that first chapter. Not just because of the power of grace but because of the nature of grace. We've defined biblical grace as "divine enablement". It is supernatural strength working through you, and grace is certainly an act of unmerited favor, but grace is not defined as unmerited favor. Got it? Ok!

What makes grace so pure is that you didn't work for it, nor could you ever be righteous enough in and of yourself in order to qualify for it. How big is the heart of Christ that before either you or I could ever know that we needed His grace He chose to die so that we could have it when we came to the revelation that we needed it. For many of us His grace worked tirelessly behind the scenes even when we didn't know we needed it. Strengthening us in our weakest times, giving us that last little "umph" needed to get over a certain hump in life.

That is a concept that is foreign to many of us as westerners. We are steeped in an "I scratch your back; you scratch mine" society. The average way of thinking, whether conscious or sub-(un)-conscious, is that the only way we can receive something is if we first qualify for it or do something for it. Many people struggle with the possibility of receiving something clear and free, no strings attached. So when it comes to God's grace no wonder many struggle with fully embracing it and properly appropriating it. We haven't earned it yet it's been given to us to access at any time, even in those times when we don't know we need to access it.

Matthew 11:29

"Take my yoke upon you, and learn of me; for I am meek and lowly in heart: and ye shall find rest unto your souls."

Matthew 11:29 accurately sums up the selfless heart of Christ concerning us. It is His desire to exchange "yokes" with us. What is a yoke? We see it referenced several times in the Bible. In Numbers 19:2 we see it referencing the curved piece of wood that is fitted on the neck of oxen for the purpose of binding them so that they could draw the plough. In Jeremiah 27:2 the word we see translated as yoke is the word "motah", which literally means a staff or bar. Both of these Hebrew words are employed figuratively of a heavy burden, severe bondage, a great affliction, and even subjection. Jesus says, "Emancipate yourself from the bondages of your life; the heavy burdens that weigh on you and give them to me." The connotation is that our daily yokes are hard task masters, heavy to carry and hard to satisfy. But He says He will trade yokes with us! He says if we give him our yokes (hard, heavy, strenuous, difficult to please), He will give us His. He paints the picture for us and says it's light, and it's easy. However, He does not stop there. He says we would find "rest for our souls". That's the seat of our desires, our emotions, hurts, pains, joys, hopes. All of those things that constantly pull on us from within, in serving Him, will come to rest.

How is this possible? When we fully yield to Christ and we fully submit ourselves to serve Him (not only as God but as Lord), He makes Himself principally responsible for us. Let's look at Matthew's gospel again.

Matthew 6:25–31
"25 "That is why I tell you not to worry about everyday life—whether you have enough food and drink, or enough clothes to wear. Isn't life more than food, and your body more than clothing? 26 Look at the birds. They don't plant or harvest or store food in barns, for your heavenly Father

35

feeds them. And aren't you far more valuable to him than they are? 27 Can all your worries add a single moment to your life? 28 "And why worry about your clothing? Look at the lilies of the field and how they grow. They don't work or make their clothing, 29 yet Solomon in all his glory was not dressed as beautifully as they are. 30 And if God cares so wonderfully for wildflowers that are here today and thrown into the fire tomorrow, he will certainly care for you. Why do you have so little faith? 31 "So don't worry about these things, saying, 'What will we eat? What will we drink? What will we wear?' 32 These things dominate the thoughts of unbelievers, but your heavenly Father already knows all your needs. 33 Seek the Kingdom of God[e] above all else, and live righteously, and he will give you everything you need."

The person who has received the "yoke of Christ" is the one that is fulfilling the mandate of verse 33. They are seeking the will of God. And what is His will? That

the yoke of bondage that you and I were born into be

broken off our lives by the power of the Cross of

Christ and being born again into the Kingdom of God.

Remember what Galatians 5:1 said?

> *Stand fast therefore in the liberty wherewith*
> *Christ hath made us free. And be not*
> *entangled again with the yoke of bondage.*

What is this yoke of bondage? Sin and death brought

on by the Law and the flesh nature. Let's consider

Romans 8:1–4

> **1. Therefore there is now no condemnation**
> **for those who are in Christ Jesus. 2. For the**
> **law of the Spirit of life in Christ Jesus has**
> **set you free from the law of sin and of**
> **death. 3. For what the Law could not do,**
> **weak as it was through the flesh, God did:**
> **sending His own son in the likeness of**
> **sinful flesh and as an offering for sin, He**
> **condemned sin in the flesh, so 4. that the**

requirement of the law might be fulfilled in us, who do not walk according to the flesh but according to the spirit.

Verse one endows us with justification. Verse two endows us with sanctification. The freedom that we receive in the second verse is the evidence of the acquittal judgment we receive in verse 1. It's not the reason we were acquitted, it is the evidence. We were not "justified' (acquitted) because of the change in our lives. Our lives have the opportunity to change because we have been justified. But we can't stop there. Verse 3 is the part where we can really start getting excited. "...he condemned sin in the flesh." What does this mean? This doesn't mean that he damns (executes condemning judgment). The law could do that and did do it. (The curse(s) came as a byproduct of the law.) That's what Deuteronomy 28:15 says in the ESV:

But if you will not obey the voice of the Lord your God, or be careful to do all His commandments and His statutes that I command you today, then all these curses shall come upon you and overtake you.

So curses were a consequence (condemnation) for sin (missing the mark). So sin was indeed damned in this sense. But Romans 8:3 starts off by setting apart the work of Christ and the work of the law by stating that He came to do what the law could not do. The law damned sin, so He had to have come to do more than that. When Paul says, "God condemned sin in the flesh," he is saying that through the life and death (flesh) of Jesus by the Cross, the final judgment was executed against the sin of everyone who is in Christ. Let me repeat that. Everyone who is IN CHRIST. That's a specificity. Not everyone can lay claim to the work of the Cross (condemnation of sin in the flesh) because not everyone is in Christ.

If there is a criminal court case that has multiple

defendants as a part of it and a judgment is issued in

that case acquitting the defendants of all charges,

then those particular defendants are acquitted. If

there were other people who had taken part in the

crime or had committed the same crime but were not

included as defendants then those other people have

not been acquitted and there is still a judgment to

come against them once they are charged. Does that

make sense? But what the preceding case with those

who were acquitted did do was establish precedence

for any future legal matters, which means when those

others are brought up on charges, if they follow the

same pattern as those gone before they too can lay

claim to the same defense and receive the same

acquittal.

I'm sure you like me have seen TV commercials

advertising class-action lawsuits against major

corporations, be they concerning asbestos, surgical meshes, or other things. When and if those cases are won, only those that submitted themselves to that law firm and made themselves claimants in that lawsuit will receive payouts from the winnings. You don't do the work though. The attorney does. All you have to do is sign up and follow the attorney's counsel.

> **Ephesians 2:8. *For it is by grace you have been saved, through faith—and this is not from yourselves (your work), it is the gift of God.***

You do not have to, nor can you work for the gift of God. It has been gifted to you as an inheritance, though it does come with prerequisites in order to receive the inheritance. Grace (divine empowerment/ God's ability working in you) is a gift freely given and part of the most dominant works of the grace of Christ is that it has redeemed us from the curse.

According to Galatians 3:13 He (Christ) redeemed us from the curse, but remember Romans 8 now; you must be IN Christ (a part of the class action lawsuit) in order to receive the payout of grace. This means this notion of "generational curses" functioning in the life of born-again believers is an antiquated, false, and misinformed teaching. If, according to Galatians 3, He became the curse in order to break the curse off of the lives of those that are in Him, how can you still be cursed ... in Him? People are often dumbfounded when I say, "THERE IS NO GENERATIONAL CURSE IN OR ON THE LIFE OF BELIEVERS."

Further on that topic, if there were generational curses on believers why didn't Jesus EVER speak to it or deal with it? Why are none of the twelve Apostles of the Lamb (the original 12) ever recorded speaking to them? Because Christ came to bring an end of them and He did. BE FREE from that notion! You are

NOT cursed because of your mother or fathers IF (condition) you are in Christ. I'm sure your mind is now racing (especially if you were raised in a Pentecostal environment, you heard the words "generational curse" in every message LOL). Well, why do you have the sicknesses your parents have/ had? Perhaps because you share in your parents' diet. They had high blood pressure, and you have it. Why? Check out your diet. Why are there certain mental illnesses in your family? Genetics, perhaps the fallen state of man. It is NOT because of a curse. You are a born-again, blood-bought believer. Christ PAID your debt in full. The curse (judgment/lien) against you was also paid for in that transaction.

Our obsession in certain sects of Pentecostalism with generational curses is nothing new. Remember in the gospel of John in the ninth chapter? There was a man that had been blind from birth.

"As Jesus was walking along, he saw a
man who had been blind from birth. 2
"Rabbi," his disciples asked him, "why was
this man born blind? Was it because of his
own sins or his parents' sins?" 3 "It was
not because of his sins or his parents'
sins," Jesus answered. "This happened so
the power of God could be seen in him. 4
We must quickly carry out the tasks
assigned us by the one who sent us.[a] The
night is coming, and then no one can work.
5 But while I am here in the world, I am the
light of the world."
John 9:1–5

Ultimately, the power in the purpose of whatever your

reality is is found in its ability to glorify God. The

disciples ebulliently assumed that a man's blindness

was the result of a generational curse—a

consequence executed on the child because of the

sin of his fathers. In His anomalistic way He dismisses

the notion and explains that it was not a result of a

curse but that the glory of God might be revealed. It takes a perspicacious person to be able see past the cloak of religious definitions and reasoning for turmoil and to be proficient in seeing an opportunity for God's grace to be evidenced. Remember now, grace is NOT defined as unmerited favor but as divine strength. Your weaknesses give an opportunity for you to exercise God's supernatural strength in order to take dominion in your life.

For some reason we have held on to and found fuel in the notion that we are cursed. Curses have become the reason we've done things or haven't done things. They've produced, endured, and maintained a culture of fear and in doing so have attempted to create a distance between the believer and the love of Christ. Now, I want you to make sure that you are being present to this reading and that you're not reading this book and these words about grace through the mind of what has become popular teaching about grace. I bring to the conversation the "Love of Christ" not as a justification to sin but as cause not to. When love is properly valued, it produces priority consideration for the giver in the heart of the receiver.

I always related the curse to my parents' belt when I was a child. My father had this old, cow-hide leather belt, the kind of belt you sharpen a razor on the back of. Engraved in that belt was his grandfather's name and that long belt hung on the back of my dad's closet door. That belt was a reminder of the consequences for disobedience. My obedience was learned by the things that I suffered. But the older I got, the less my father would physically discipline me. Not that my father whipped me often as it was. Yet, as I grew older it wasn't the belt that kept me in line; it was my valuing my father's provision, care, protection, and selflessness that kept me in line. This value produced a sense of honor so that I did not want to communicate to him that I devalued him. So I made sure (for the most part, ha) that I did all that I could to support him and to be a son that he could be proud of.

You see, honor is the consciousness of men of integrity. The older I grew the more I wanted to show my honor. The belt brought fear as a child and instilled obedience. But with the belt there were times I'd do things I really didn't want to do, but because of the fear of the belt I did them.

This is how many people are going through life in their relationship with God. They are doing things they've been told to do, but their heart isn't in those actions. They're tithing out of fear, going to church out of obligation, serving out of habit. Though they are doing all of the things a good Christian is supposed to do, many aren't seeing the response they expect. I submit to you that the reason is because these things are being done in fear, and not in honor. The hand is complying but the heart is not with it. Do you know it's possible to do the right thing and still not be pleasing to God? All of your human virtues and self- goodness are displeasing to God.

That's what Paul points out in Romans 14:23 when he says, "Whatever is not from faith is sin." A wise act that is faithless does not glorify God no matter how much it may benefit you. He points this out in the 20th verse as he says, ***"Abraham grew strong in his faith as he gave glory to God."*** If the source of your strength and growth is not your faith then it's not bringing glory to God. As Kingdom citizens we are encouraged to do everything to the glory of God in 1

Corinthians 10:31. If our obedience is a product of fear, rather than of faith, it is not honor nor does it communicate trust. Christ comes and brings an end to the curse, putting the belt away, and calls us to maturity.

In my book *The Order of Inheritance* I talk about the transition from the old covenant as (mere) servants to the new covenant as sons and friends. A good father is not looking to strike fear in the heart of his sons. Rather his fathering produces honor, commands reverence, and finally installs a consideration for the will of the father in the heart of sons.

> **Romans 8:17**
> **Now if we are children, then we are heirs—heirs of God and co-heirs with Christ...**

Beloved, you are an heir and a joint heir. God's greatest desire for and from you is for your love and admiration that produces a lifestyle of honor. When

49

you honor someone, you consider their predilections, and, yes, live your life in a way that makes adjustments so as not to offend them. Not because you think they're going to beat you, but you simply do not desire to be a source of pain or hurt in their lives. You can love freely and purely when there's no threat of a curse lingering over your head. Are you still struggling to believe you can't be cursed?

Let's consider this.

> **Romans 5:13**
> **To be sure, sin was in the world before the law was given, but sin is not charged against anyone's account where there is no law.**

In other words sin was not counted as a sin because there was not yet any law to break. Imagine driving on the German autobahn at 100 miles an hour. You don't have to fear getting a speeding ticket because there is no speed limit. Now, wisdom will teach you it's probably not considerable or honorable of your life or the lives of others to put them so recklessly at risk, but there won't be a judgment if you do. Now imagine a new governmental leader comes to power who institutes a speed limit (law). Their purpose might be to teach people how dangerous their driving is, and so by instituting a speed limit they protect them from their own destruction. Then a new leader is elected who removes this law and removes this speed limit. There's no more speed limit so there is no more infraction.

Romans 4:15
Because the law brings wrath. And where there is no law there is no transgression.

So if you're struggling with the notion that there is no more curse, your real struggle is whether or not the (Mosaic) law is still in effect. If you're struggling with that question the real struggle is whether or not you believe in the finished work of the cross. Consider Jesus' own words in Matthew 5:17. He said, *"Do not think that I have come to abolish the law, I have not come to abolish them, but to fulfill them."* If in fact Jesus did fulfill the (Mosaic) law, we that are in Christ don't owe the law any further payments. If He fulfilled the law and the curse came as a consequence of the law, then He's also dealt with the curse.

Many people oftentimes don't realize the measure of dishonor they display by continuing to believe that they that are in Christ can still be cursed. What you're saying when you believe this is "The power of Adam's sin is greater than the power of Christ's (the second Adam) work.. Vs. 12 of Romans 5 says, *"Therefore, just as sin entered the world through one man, and death through sin, so also death was passed on to all men..."* But now let's look at **Romans 8:2:** *"because through Christ Jesus, the law of the spirit who gives life has set you free from the law of sin and death."*

Who is "the spirit who gives life"? Christ is. What is "the law of the spirit who gives life?" LOVE! He desires your love, which is a demonstration of honor. Your measure of freedom is based on your measure of honor. See you cannot honor the finished work of Christ and choose to remain bound to the control of a curse. He died that you might be free. The least that you could do is BE FREE!

Chapter 7 of Hebrews is one of my favorites. Look at this:

> *Vs. 11 "So if the priesthood of Levi, on which the law was based, could have achieved the perfection God intended, why*

did God need to establish a different priesthood, with a priest in the order of Melchizedek instead of the order of Levi and Aaron? 12. And if the priesthood is changed, THE LAW MUST ALSO BE CHANGED TO PERMIT IT."

Do you see that? THE LAW HAS BEEN CHANGED! And the curse being a product of the law means that the curse has been lifted. We have gone from curse to covering and cure. The cure for the law of sin and death was the cross, which allowed us the permit to take dominion in the stead of Christ. This restored dominion is the gift of God to us as His children. He has reconciled us back to the dominion mandate through the death of Christ according to Colossians 1:22. The sins of your father, and your father's father do not rest upon you. The closest concept of a curse that you'll find in the New Testament is the word "anathema" in Galatians 1:8–9. This word in Greek means something that is devoted to destruction or to bring judgment upon oneself. A curse is an imprecation of evil, and a judgment is systematic consequences for one's own action.

I.e.: If you run out into the highway and get hit by a car, that was not a curse. Your own actions brought their own judgment. There are certain choices that we can make that carry a judgment with them; however, this is not to be confused with God cursing you. The Mosaic Law being fulfilled does not cease the government of spiritual law and laws of nature. If you get on top of a high building and jump, your own actions will judge you according to the law of gravity. What goes up must come down. If you live a reckless life there are indeed consequences that come by reason of those actions, but not by reason of God releasing a curse against you.

Paul says if you choose to live under the law of sin and death (thus no longer hidden behind the cross) you will live under a curse according to Galatians 3:10.

> **"For as many as are of the works of the law are under the curse..."**

Not only has Christ freed you from the curse but from the law of sin and death. Why choose to live a life of sin when you have access to the divine grace (divine ability) to live above the government of the flesh?

> 2 Corinthians 7:1 **Having therefore these promises, dearly beloved, let us cleanse ourselves from all filthiest of the flesh and spirit, perfecting holiness in reverence for God.**

Since God has given us this gift (promise) in grace, the least that we can do is dedicate our lives back to Him and commit to living above the filth of the flesh in order to perfect holiness (being set apart or dedicated). Why do this? Not out of fear but out of reverence for the Lord. To show Him our appreciation and our desire to be like him. Charles Caleb Colton, the English cleric and writer, said that "the most sincere form of flattery is emulation." Flatter God by striving to be like Him. Show Him your appreciation for His finished work by living a life as unto the Lord.

NO! You cannot repay Him. But you can demonstrate your appreciation for your gift, God's grace. You are no longer cursed! Dispatch that stronghold from your heart and mind and live free. Not just free from the fear of the curse, but live free from a life of sin.

Grace has not freed you to sin. It has freed you from sin. Sin is a yoke that binds. You no longer have to be bound in that yoke. Christ our King has volunteered to exchange yokes with you. However, this gift of grace must be received in order to partake of it. It is freely available to you, but you must "take it" upon you. That's an action. The notion that you are covered in grace even if you don't receive the giver of grace is deception.

If I give you a gift and you leave it wrapped up and never open it the gift will never benefit you even though I gave it to you. Even as you read this book take up the gift of grace! Choose not to live a life of weaknesses. You've been given access to His strength.

Chapter Three

The Inner Work for Outward Change

The true work of grace begins deep within our heart, soul, and spirit. It is not solely some macho display of bravado that feels some sense of self-gratification in being free to sin. Actually quite to the contrary; we see grace most prominently in the lives of men and women with broken spirits and contrite hearts. Remember 2 Corinthians 12:9 says that His strength [grace] is made perfect in our weakness.

People who function in the most grace must equally realize they are the most undeserving. And in that realization He releases more grace.

> *James 4:6 "But He give the more grace. Wherefore he said, God resisteth the proud, but give the grace unto the humble."*

Grace is not a result of giftedness or anointing but of humility. That's a powerful statement. He gives more grace to the humble. It is therefore important that we understand humility. This is to be postured under a sense of our own ignorance and weakness. Knowing that we only know what we know and, even in that, finding no comfort in the shadows of knowing that there is so much more to know. Arrogance is the result of an inflated sense of reality, when you are so intoxicated with what you know that you are blinded to the reality of His omniscience. No matter how much you or I know it is but a fragmented fragment of the magnanimity of His knowledge, knowledge so vast that there are no words within our reach capable of defining the dimensions of it. Understand that in order to be able to accurately define a thing you must find language that is not itself a part of that which you attempt to define.

This is one of the greatest struggles of our humanity, the attempt to see a God outside of our own humanity though through human lenses. When we consider all of the verbiage we have about God, it is a paled attempt at accurately describing a God we don't have

the capacity to accurately describe. So we resort to

our human understandings. "The hand of God; God

walking through the garden; God said..." All things we

say of God yet we must realize these are but poor

translations of our experiences with God. He doesn't

have hands, nor does He walk, nor does He need a

mouth in order to speak. But we are humans so we

define him out of our analogy of human life. Those are

our experiences and so we anachronistically say them

of the Lord God. God cannot be confined to the

barriers and dimensions of our very limited human

language(s).

David understood this humility as he felt small as a

"worm" (before God) in consideration of his self-

diminishing faults. Even that description, though

humbling to us, is still arrogant; an assumption that

we could actually know the size of God in order to run

a comparison between us and Him. However, we must resolve to our best language and be humbled in knowing our best still plummets to the depths of inadequacy. At the acceptance of that truth you are then positioned to fall back on the grace of God. Suffice it to say that few people reach the depth of that understanding. As a result we have a culture replete with ignorant arrogance, so assured of ourselves without being slightly conscious to the possibility that our assurance is in and of itself unsecured.

> *Isaiah 64:6 But we are all as an unclean thing, and all our righteousnesses are as filthy rags; and we all do fade as a leaf; and our iniquities, like the wind, have taken us away.*

That is an accurate description and depiction of our truth. As we descend into the depths of our existential nature, into the core of our being, into the reality of our soul, it is there we identify our greatest weakness to be our human existence. As we accept that, the true work can begin. Part of the handicapping nature of our sight is that if not properly directed we will allow visual sight to become our first line of judgment. If what we see is where we lay our hats then it will subsequently be where we do our most work.

The poverty of our humanity is exposed when we resort to surface modifications with no existential transformation. Romans 12:2 is, in my opinion, a life-giving passage of scripture. It is a road map on "where" to start in order to finish.

> *Romans 12:2 But be not conformed to this world, but be ye transformed by the renewing of your mind...*

The mind—the Greek word "nous"—differs greatly from our brain. The mind is our faculty of perception and cognitive ability inclusive of our feelings, determinations, and ability to reason. That is where the true work must begin. Everything about our true selves is result of the mind and, deeper still, a result of the soul's influence upon the mind. So, even before we begin to work on our minds we need to turn to the soul.

The soul is the seat of desires, emotions, and your will. It is where pains, disappointments, joys, and frustrations are housed. It is the soul that opens the gateway to certain spiritual bondages that attach themselves to certain emotional dispositions. The average person goes through life living as a soul. Though many use the words "soul" and "spirit" interchangeably we understand that they are not synonyms and are not the same. You are a spirit, you live in a body, and you have a soul. These are important distinctions so that you can understand the tripartite nature of man. Though the various aspects of your being are distinct those aspects cannot exist in the Earth realm independent of themselves. Distinct but indivisible; who does that sound like? God! God has revealed Himself to us as Father, Son, and Holy Spirit. Though each is distinct, their eternal existence requires coexistence in eternal harmony.

Through the multi-part process of salvation, regeneration, justification, and sanctification, the spirit of God begins to take up habitation in your spirit. Herein begins the internal conflict, the war between natures, because, remember, the average one of us lives life through the soul until we receive the Holy Spirit. Contrary to our exaggerated sense of salvation every aspect of you is NOT changed and is NOT regenerated. There are many "saved people" who are conflicted. Confused even. On our journey through the process of salvation, and as aspects of our selves come into conflict with our knowledge of Him, His will, and His way, a decision must be made—a decision to either deny His will or to deny our own.

Without a proper understanding that there is, in fact, a process to and through salvation it will be easy to grow discouraged and progress through this process in acrimony. Salvation is God's provision for the reality of our humanity, a reality that finds us all born in sin and shaped in iniquity. Grace is God's "child support plan" designed to assist us through this lifelong process. Seeing grace in this light, a dichotomy is presented. Grace produces the unction that draws us to God and simultaneously is the strength that enables us to be committed in our pursuit of God. It is grace that allows us the equanimity necessary to hold the course of this process.

Regeneration becomes the gateway to the new life of the spirit man. It is only spirit that can give life (birth) to spirit. Pursuit of spirit life is not to be simply spiritually gregarious, some temporary attempt to engage the life that spirit provides without any commitment to the nature of such an awakening. However, such a commitment is necessary in order to enter into the Kingdom of God (John 3:5). Remember the Bible account of Nicodemus found there in John 3?

> *(Amplified Version) 1. Now there was a certain man among the Pharisees named Nicodemus, a ruler (member of the Sanhedrin) among the Jews, 2 who came to Jesus at night and said to Him, "Rabbi (Teacher), we know [without any doubt] that You have come from God as a teacher; for no one can do these signs [these wonders, these attesting miracles] that You do unless God is with him." 3 Jesus answered him, "I*

assure you and most solemnly say to you, unless a person is born again [reborn from above—spiritually transformed, renewed, sanctified], he cannot [ever] see and experience the kingdom of God." 4 Nicodemus said to Him, "How can a man be born when he is old? He cannot enter his mother's womb a second time and be born, can he?" 5 Jesus answered, "I assure you and most solemnly say to you, unless one is born of water and the Spirit he cannot [ever] enter the kingdom of God. 6 That which is born of the flesh is flesh [the physical is merely physical], and that which is born of the Spirit is spirit.

Nicodemus was a learned man and one who like his fellow Pharisees had developed a sense of self-righteousness. As he begins to hear Jesus preaching the gospel of the Kingdom he's intrigued. The question he poses in the fourth verse is not literal. He was really saying, "I'm sure you don't mean literally, so what is it that you're saying?" Nicodemus was familiar with the colloquialism "born again". Ellicott's *Commentary for English Readers* says, "The thought is not wholly strange to him. The rabbis were accustomed to speak of proselytism as children, and the term "new creature" was in frequent use to express the call of Abraham." Nicodemus' confusion is in that he has already responded to the call of Abraham. How could he be born again after already being born again?

Jesus is of course not talking about a new natural life, nor simply answering the "call of Abraham". He's talking a new personal start. If someone were to ask us the meaning of life we'd get several different meanings. Some might respond with an abstract definition. Pulling on a broader view, someone else might refer to their children, their spouse, or their purpose. Life cannot simply be defined as the heart that beats within our chest or the blood that flows through our veins. With such an infinitesimal view of life many questions are opened up. If that is the meaning of life then how is it that one man who is shot in the stomach and loses a certain amount of blood dies and another with a similar wound and similar blood loss lives? We must take a more idiosyncratic approach. Life is to each of us individual and is spiritual. As we tap into this spirit-experienced life and unlock the liberating power of the law of the spirit of life, those things that seemed to control your life lose their grip on you.

Romans 8:14 KJV
For if you live according to human nature, you are going to die, but if by the spirit you continuously put to death the activities of the body you will live.

So if life is to be long lasting and satisfying it must be spirit-life, a life that defies the gravitational pull of our socio-economic cultures, the pull to be like everyone else, to think like the status quo, and to live from the outside in. Like the gravitational pull of the natural atmosphere, though difficult, you can break free of its control. This is not easy as it seems natural to us to live from the outside in, taking on the ideologies, philosophies, and mentalities of our pseudo realities and societies. Like an airplane you must defy these weights in order to elevate into dimensions not common to man. In order for an aircraft to take flight it has to defy the principal forces of weight and drag. Weight is what works to pull the airplane back to the ground. Some of the ideologies, philosophies, and mentalities of your life become weights. The experiences of your natural reality and their impressions on your psyche endeavor to give the soulish aspect of you dominion over your flesh, thus subjecting your spirit to be in the back seat.

Defying weight in and of itself is not enough however. You've got to also defy drag. Consider the various nuances of your life, the appetites, desires, and lusts that attempt to drag your soul and flesh into a way of living far too low for someone of your high call. Weight and drag can only be overcome by lift, and it is lift that then takes the plane into the air. An environment of faith and consistent voices of faith serve as the catalyst of lift. However, those external deposits are only as effective as they are sealed in the soil of your spirit. The "activities" of your body are the weights that endeavor to ground the potential flight of your spirit. Endeavoring, however, to bring correction to yourself by external means is temporary at best.

Remember you began as spirit, your primary nature is spirit, and the strongest aspect of you is spirit. In that light it is your spirit man that must become ground zero for your work. It's easy to make changes obvious to sensory perception. Changing your clothes, where you live, even your disposition is all external work. None of these things, though, are driving forces in your life. The driving forces, or the spirit, of your life are identified in the "whys" of your life. Rather than focusing on what you wear take some time and consider what's under that. What's the reason and the feelings attached to that external manifestation?

Rather than focusing on emotions and feelings take the time to look under them. What's driving them and producing them? How you feel is important, but why you feel how you feel is even more important. Why do certain situations in your life produce certain feelings, and why do you feel the way you do about those feelings? What's the mentality being associated with that feeling even subconsciously? Let's say you've got a major project going on at work and usually major projects are major stress factors in your life. Your subconscious is automatically going to assume that this project is going to be stressful, and then your body is going to react to that impending stress. Pause to consider that grace hasn't been factored into the equation. If grace is divine enablement, the strength of God working through you, then your capacity has got to be considered based on His abilities and not your own.

Certainly His strengths are greater than yours, and the omnipotent God cannot be overwhelmed by trivial matters in the earth. So through His grace what was stressful to you can suddenly become just another day's work. The feelings of anxiety, negative attitudes, and intensified engagements that came as a result of that stress have also now been brought under control.

It is through the word of faith and understanding of the gospel of the Kingdom that the peace, serenity, and stability that you are in pursuit of cease to just be theory. They become actual targets, goals, and marks that you shoot for. The usual disappointing realities of your day-to-day life become out of bounds for you. They become unacceptable.

> *1 John 3:9*
>
> *Whosoever is born of God doth not commit sin; for His seed remaineth in Him; and he cannot sin, because he is born of God.*

Being born of the spirit is the process in which the driving force of your life changes, once driven by money, people, and other selfish desires; now being driven by the will of God, fulfilling His divine purpose in the earth. When the seed of the word truly takes root in you, the Bible says you sin no more. Now

pause for a moment and expand your perception of

sin. It's not just lascivious living, promiscuity, or the

like. Sin here is the Greek word "hamartano", which

means to miss the mark. When you are born again,

those new targets (marks) have developed. Now

living beneath those marks becomes sin. Having a

good day becomes a target and having a bad one

becomes sin. "Do you mean it's my fault if I have a

bad day?" Yes! You may not be able to control what

goes on in your day. But you do have the power to

control (through the grace of Christ) how it influences

your being.

When in your way of thinking it becomes dishonorable

to engage in certain things, respond in certain ways,

you'll begin to see it as sin. When walking in harmony

with your faith is of principal importance to you, sin is

not an acceptable place to live in. Romans 14

declared that anything that is not in faith is sin. So then faith is the mark. That is the target! What then is faith? I've defined faith as total confidence. Take, for example, you've been taught the color blue. No matter how many times someone tells you blue is red, you will be unfazed because you are convinced you know what blue is. You won't lose any sleep over what they've said; you won't feel uneasy about what you know because you are convinced and have total confidence.

That's how faith should affect your life. When you are in faith, anything that contradicts your faith is beneath your mark. Adam and Eve's sin was the result of a lack of faith. Had they been convinced that they were "in the image and likeness of God" the enemy would not have been able to provoke the response that resulted in the fallen state of man. Eating the fruit was a response to being unconvinced. The devil told them they would be like God. They believed that. The truth was they already were like Him and didn't need to receive anything else to be like Him.

The enemy's focus is to talk you out of the things that you are supposed to be convinced of in faith. If he can talk you out of your standing in God he can produce adverse responses in you, responses like worry and doubt, fear and depression, anger and a lack of integrity, rejection resulting in promiscuity. Hold your faith! Total confidence is the mark. Not total confidence in the situations or situations of life but total confidence in the God of the universe. If your faith is placed in anything that is changeable, moveable, and subject to the changes of life your faith is one situation away from failing. Your faith must be placed in an immutable source.

Hebrews 12:2 KJV

Looking unto Jesus the author and finisher of our faith; who for the joy that was set before him endured the cross, despising the shame, and is set down at the right hand of the throne of God.

When you've got a clear focus on the object of your faith and a proper understanding of your purpose, then the various "crosses" of your life no longer produce the emotions and reactions they once did. Jesus is the object of our faith. It is His grace that we must learn to live through. His grace (strength) has more than proven itself. Do you have any other examples of one temporarily relinquishing the full measure of their divine power, choosing to become human, being crucified, rising, and still being able to function in perfect love for those who did all of this to Him? Well, that's grace (divine strength) that has more than proven itself.

This consciousness is one that has to be developed from the inside out. External alterations are futile without true internal convictions. Your responses to life are simply manifestations of your chosen internal focus.

Faith focuses can only produce faith responses. Emotional focuses can only produce emotional responses. If you focus only on surface work you'll only reap surface results. Faith doesn't work from the surface level. It is the opposite of a life controlled by the senses. 2 Corinthians 5 reminds us that believers live by faith and not by the senses. The word "live" is the Greek word "peripateo" and it means "to regulate one's life." When you live or walk by faith, it means you are regulated by faith. The life of the spirit man is sourced and strengthened by the Spirit.

By resorting to the government of the soul (emotions) or of the flesh (lusts) you declare independence from the spirit. You can't reap the benefits of a spirit-led life from a soul-governed mind or a flesh-controlled appetite. You have the power to choose to exist from a higher place and plane. Defy the gravitational pull of the weights of sin and the drag of the flesh. Do the inner work, and the outer change will be inevitable.

Chapter Four

Conquering Conformation

It is difficult to be truly authentic in a world of relativity, a world where the differences between up and down are not absolute. A world where we say we "don't want to be defined by labels" and so any definitive truths about ourselves are shunned. A world where the scholars, and now some [false] religious extremists, have made it seem as though nothing is absolute. The paradigm is that we can all be right. Anything can be right and nothing wrong. This synthetic paradigm is hidden in some false reverence of the magnanimity of God, the belief that because God is so big there can be nothing that exists that is not in agreement with Him.

The Family Policy Institute of Washington conducted a survey on the campus of the University of Washington. The focus of the survey was to identity absolutes as they relate to identity. The interviewer was a short white man. As he began to ask questions of random students the conflict became clear. These supposedly educated students could not be absolute, definitive, or objective.

He asked one young lady, "What if I told you I was a woman?"

She responded, "I'd say great and embrace you as a woman."

He then asked, "What if I told you I was a tall Chinese woman?"

She paused for a moment and said, "Well, I don't have the right to tell you who you are, so then you must be a tall Chinese woman."

This line of questioning went on throughout the day with several random students and few of them could be objective. Though it was obvious that he was a short white male in his true self they could not, or would not, identify that. It was more comfortable to accept what was inauthentic (if it meant not ruffling any feathers) than it was to communicate the authentic truth.

Is authenticity being relatively original or is the scale of originality based on the master plan and original intent of the creator? Creation has never had the power to define itself. The fact that it is a creation suggests that it was created in order to fulfill a set intent, purpose, and definition. Not the other way around. The creation doesn't lead to the definition. The definition leads to the creation. The creation is the offspring and the product of the definition. Its purpose for being is sourced out of the definition.

Without clear perspective of absolute definitions it is impossible to identify whether or not something is being properly appropriated or not. Without being able to identify whether or not it is being properly appropriated it becomes impossible to troubleshoot when things go wrong. In order to identify a malfunction I first have to identify the function. Before any inventor builds their invention they first decide what problem the invention is going to solve. Then they draw up a plan in order to design a prototype of the specific design that has been designed in order to solve a specific problem or meet a specific need.

To use a creation in a way other than it was originally intended to be used is to pervert the creation. Though we usually think something sexual when we think about perversion, perversion has a much wider meaning than that. Using the tail end of a screwdriver to pound in a nail is to pervert the screwdriver. You have a divine purpose in the earth. You were created for a specific purpose in time. To lend yourself to an existence independent of the original intent of the creator is to lend yourself to perversion.

> **Proverbs 19:21 NIV: "Many are the plans in a person's heart, but it is the LORD's purpose that prevails."**

Ontologically we reach our highest level of existence when we tap into the purpose our creator had in mind for us before the creation of the time in which we exist. Perversion was at the root of Lucifer's expulsion from heaven. Lucifer's very name from the Hebrew word "helel" means brightness. He's called the "morning star" and in Isaiah he's called the "son of Dawn." Though Isaiah 14 is talking about the king of Babylon it is more clearly focused on the spirit and demonic power behind this king. Ezekiel 28 says that he was "the anointed cherub." Without getting off into angel-ology, cherubs are the angels that are closest to God's throne. They are the guardians of His presence and unapproachable light. He was the cherub of cherubs. No higher assignment existed, but Lucifer despised it. His purpose was to protect the presence of God, but he attempted to exalt his purpose above the purpose for which he was created. As he crossed into this perversion of purpose he was immediately expelled from heaven.

Through Christ Jesus we have been given the rights to be seated in heavenly places with Him. However, the fulfillment of original intents, divine purpose, and the will of God is necessary to exercise the authority of such a high and lofty seat. That task (fulfilling original intents) is one of the most difficult tasks one will ever undertake. The journey first begins by identifying the difference between what you want to be and do and what God wants you to be and do.

We are raised being influenced concerning who and what we should be. We're taught "you can be whatever you want to be." Perhaps you were raised to "walk in your parents' footsteps" or to take over the family business. Beyond being impressed on about what we should be we are constantly being shaped into the "hows" of our ways of being. Without conscious work to resist the gravitational pull of our environment we are constantly becoming like the ways of the people around us. If you're raised around hypersensitive and super-emotional people you'll likely be hypersensitive and super-emotional. If you're raised around people who reject emotions, deny them and suppress them, that'll likely be who you become. This ongoing molding doesn't only happen as children but well into our adulthood. You are constantly being shaped and pressed upon, slowly conforming to the likeness of your environment.

1 Corinthians 15:3

Do not be misled: "Bad company corrupts good character."

The principal example is the story of Adam and Eve. Adam is fulfilling purpose, and the Lord gives him Eve. Together they have a corporate purpose that they begin to fulfill. Eve is then persuaded by Satan to commit the same treason he committed. He persuades her to attempt to elevate herself and her actions above the purpose and will of God. Adam is in hearing range and is impressed upon to follow suit. After they "fall into sin" they attempt to "cover their nakedness." They attempt to use their own intellect to cover themselves, and then they try to hide from the Lord. They put on pieces of their environment (the leaves of the tree). This is the ultimate goal of the enemy. His goal and desire is to see us make decisions that dishonor God. Like Adam it's almost

91

second nature to fall back on our own reasoning and finally attempt to separate ourselves from God.

He (Satan) has no authority in our lives as long as we are walking in integrity and in line with God's divine will and plan for our lives. If he can cause us to break integrity with our word and then break integrity with the will of God for our lives, he has already got one of our feet into the conformation trap. When we think of something being pure, we think of it being untouched, original and authentically what it was made and intended to be. The dictionary defines pure as *"not mixed or adulterated with any other substance or material."* When something is pure, it's not contaminated by environment or conditions. It is untouched and unaltered.

However, on the contrary, when something is polluted, it has been altered from its original state. It has conformed to the presence of whatever pollutant was introduced. It begins to warp and make way for whatever foreign subject has been introduced. The law of displacement is that no two things can occupy the same space at the same time. So when something contrary to the original design is introduced then whatever was in the place that the foreign subject now holds is no longer in that place. Innocence is forced out by the introduction of folly. Purity is forced out by the introduction of pollutants. The original design of the master designer is forced out by alterations of environments that are themselves designs of the master designer.

We must begin to see God as more than just a deity who sits in a lofty place in the skies above. We must see Him as a master architect, a builder of builders. Architects function off of master plans and patterns. A pattern is defined according to *Collins Dictionary* as "a model proposed for imitation." You must see yourself as a pattern that was created by a master architect. You are a model proposed for imitation; thus becoming a product of your environment completely contradicts your innate purpose. You are to be copied and because of this you must live your life in a way that follows the pattern of the master architect. A simple deviation can cause countless deviations in the environment that is designed to take its cues from you.

Knowing that this would be hard work—having to live life as a model and as a pattern—God Himself came and gave us a pattern for being a pattern. In the person of Jesus Christ He showed us how to take dominion rather than being dominated. He showed us how to "be in the world, but not of it." This is a concept that escapes the average individual. The average person feels they are justified in being who they are (or are not) based on where they've come

from and what they've gone through. Our society

expects us to conform to our "realities" and those who

do not are considered anomalies. "I am not a product

of my environment. My environment is a product of

my presence" has been a mantra that I've lived my

life by.

> **Romans 12:2**
> **And be not conformed to this world: but be**
> **ye transformed by the renewing of your**
> **mind, that we may prove what is that good,**
> **and acceptable, and Percy will of God.**

It is clear in the above passage of scripture that

maintaining integrity with one's authenticity is

necessary to "prove" and receive the perfect will of

God. Oftentimes we think that God's will for our life is

automatic and that it will automatically manifest. That

just is not the case. God's will for us is assigned to a

specific, divine version of ourselves. Remember when Adam and Eve ate the fruit (a false word) in the Garden of Eden? What was the first question that the Lord God asked them? "Where art thou?" (Genesis 3:9). Had God lost Adam? Of course not. Was God asking Adam to give Him his location as though he didn't already know it? Of course not! "Where art THOU?" Where are YOU? "Where is the you I created?" is the real question. Adam had lost himself and had conformed to the will, perceptions, and impressions of his environment and the world's mind that existed within it. You cannot both be authentically you and be who the serpents of your life tell you that you are. You must choose! Above both your will and the will of others for you should be the will of God. What is God's will for you? The average person rarely pauses to assess their pursuits and ensure that those pursuits are in line with God's will for them. We normally have it backwards. We try to force our will and pursuits on the will of God. Children are rarely raised being taught to make God's will priority and even beyond that how to truly identify the will of God by the word of God. As a consequence we grow up with subjective views of self, purpose, and pursuits. The American dream of being anything you want to be. This is indeed an American concept. However, it is not a Kingdom concept. Citizens of a Kingdom make the furtherance, advancement, and supreme good of the Kingdom their priority, especially those born to nobility. They are raised with the good of the Kingdom in mind. "Noblesse oblige" is a French phrase that means "nobility obligates." More than our entitlements as the children of God, as sons and daughters of the King, we have social responsibilities that we are obligated to fulfill.

Think about a prince in a kingdom and imagine that prince being given the life their station provides. But imagine that prince never being taught work ethics or to do good towards those around him and under him. Imagine that prince only experienced getting and was never taught the responsibility of giving. We would consider that prince to be spoiled and a dictator in the making.

That, however, is often our relationship with God our King. We want Him to give to us, bless us, and favor us, yet our responsibility is a distant back seat passenger to the drive of our own appetites. Such a prince is not ready to rule a kingdom. Nobility has the responsibility to conduct themselves in a way that conforms to their position and status of their seat. Not the other way around. Their presence dictates to the environment. Have you ever been in a place when a king was scheduled to visit or perhaps a presidential visit? The environment is changed to give way for the presence of a ruler. In the same way the ruler too has to conduct himself in a way indicative of his office. Every decision, stop, and conversation has to be handled with a clear view of his assignment in mind.

You are a ruler and you must carry yourself in such a way that commands the environment around you. This can be a heavy burden to live out if you do not take on the strength of the relationship that has afforded you the responsibility. What I mean is learning to borrow from the longevity of those gone on before you. If they could make it and live up to their authentic purpose in the earth SO CAN YOU!

There are two kinds of people in life. There are trailblazers and then there are pathfinders. Which are you? Obviously, trailblazers make the trails and pathfinders find the trails that the trailblazers blazed.

All of us are part trailblazer and part pathfinder. If you're too much of a trailblazer you'll find yourself wasting time recreating what has already been created. If you're too much of a pathfinder you'll never leave your individual fingerprint on the world. Use the wisdom of those around you, but maintain your fingerprint.

The Bible tells a story of David and Goliath in 1 Samuel 17. The history says that Goliath had intimidated the armies of the Lord and David happened to show up. He did not show up with Goliath in mind. He was on a different assignment, but when he saw and heard of what Goliath was doing, his divine purpose woke up in him. He spoke with King Saul, and Saul tried to dress David in his armor.

1 Samuel 17:39
And David girded his sword upon his armour, and he assayed to go; for he had

100

not proved it. And David said unto Saul, I
cannot go with these; for I have not proved
them. And David put them off him.

So though David was about to follow in the path of a warrior (pathfinder) he had to do it in his own way (trailblazer). Had David gone into battle wearing Saul's armor it would've been Saul's fingerprint on the victory. (Armor covered the soldiers' faces/ identities in that day.) When you conform to environments and paradigms that have not been assigned by God to shape you, you are allowing your fingerprint to be wiped away. It is the will of God that you do not conform but you transform and you be a transformer. Transformation, however, is only possible by ongoing mind renewal, a refreshing of our perspectives ensuring that we don't lose sight of our specific purpose. If everyone is doing the same thing someone is unnecessary.

Now please know I am not talking about just being contrary. There's nothing more annoying to me than someone who chooses the opposite of what everyone else chooses just to choose the opposite. Everyone says red but they say blue, not because they have an affinity towards it but simply because they didn't want to say what everyone else had said. That is as inauthentic as the person who says red just because everyone else said it. Authenticity is not just about being true to you but about being true to the master plan for you. Understand and distinguish that difference! Being true to you is not always the same as being true to the master plan for you. Who holds the master plan? The master. God our Father. The King of Kings. So in order to be true to pure authenticity you've got to keep His will central to your focus.

Oftentimes we are as guilty of changing and forcing our opinions onto our true authentic selves as others are. Huh? That's right! You have no more right to change the master plan than anyone else does. You simply have more responsibility to protect the authenticity than others do. You are the custodian and steward but you too have to give attention to the master plan if you desire to see the intended end result.

I often see people who want God's best for them but want to do it their own way. It just doesn't work like that. If you want the picture you saw you are going to have to follow the directions that come along with it. You are going to have to give heed to the contractors that work along with the architect. Contractors like mentors, spiritual advisors, and the like; those who have no personal motive other than seeing the design of the master builder come to life. And you'll have to trust those contractors to know their work. You'll have to yield to their wisdom and experience even above your own at times if you are going to walk into the reality of the model you saw.

You are fearfully and wonderfully made. Don't dishonor that by making alterations to His plans for you.

Have you ever been to a fine five-star restaurant? The chef gets offended if you try to add or take anything away from the plate. Why? Because he's already made it perfect. There's no greater plane upon which the King's Dominion is made evident than in the life of a person fully and totally submitted to His will for their life. Submitted to the degree that their language communicates submission, their goals reflect it, and their accomplishments reveal it. Be that submitted one allowing His kingdom to come in you, on Earth, as it is heaven. There's no greater sense of fulfillment for the disciplined than knowing that they did it according to the pattern. Knowing they fought the urge to take shortcuts and to make alterations. The realization that they trusted the wisdom of the master planner to have foreseen anything that could come up and that they'd already factored in provisions for the unexpected in life.

I believe that you are the one in your "world" called to authenticity. To be the difference. To stand out as one committed and convicted about being who, what, when, and where the Lord has called you to be. Receive the grace to be just that, now! Don't become another perpetuator of the lie "I did my best and that's all that matters." I don't mean if you in fact did do the best (absolute) you possibly could but if you did "your best" (subjective). What is the difference?

> ### Genesis 4:3–7
>
> *3 And in process of time it came to pass, that Cain brought of the fruit of the ground an offering unto the Lord. 4 And Abel, he also brought of the firstlings of his flock and of the fat thereof. And the Lord had respect unto Abel and to his offering: 5 But unto Cain and to his offering he had not respect. And Cain was very wroth, and his countenance fell. 6 And the Lord said unto Cain, Why art thou wroth? and why is thy countenance fallen? 7 If thou doest well, shalt thou not be accepted? and if thou doest not well, sin lieth at the door. And unto thee shall be his desire, and thou shalt rule over him.*

The story of Cain and Abel makes the difference between "I did my best" and "I did the best I possibly could" very clear. The biblical narrative begins by saying "in the process of time" (vs. 3). We don't know how much time that is as there is not enough

information to deduce this from the text. We certainly

know, however, that time has gone by. So let's say it's

20 years that have gone by. Cain and Abel both

present themselves to give God an offering.

Though there are many definitions for the word

offering *(Hebrew word minchah-strongs Hebrew*

4503), the definition here would be a gift, something

that is freely given.

A gift differs from a **sacrifice** (another definition for

the word) in that a sacrifice is something that is given

by blood. Today, it's not meant to be taken in the

literal sense but in the figurative one. Something that

cost you your "blood, sweat, and tears." A gift differs

from a **tribute** (another definition for the word) in that

a tribute is a payment that is owed to a higher-ranking

person. A gift is freely given, not commanded, and not

a recompense for sin. Even though it was freely given "of the heart", God rejects Cain's offering.

One of the most famous lines given today by persons who may not have reached a given standard is "God knows my heart." This is truer than most know. Why would God reject Cain's offering if it was from the heart? He gave it. No one forced him. There was no command, and still it was rejected.

Cain's offering was rejected because it did not meet God's standard. No, not in terms of an amount or even a type of offering. Though Cain gave a fruit and grain offering and Abel gave an animal offering that is not what's important. In vs. 4 the Bible says, "Abel gave the **firstling** of his flock, and the **fat** thereof." He gave both a quantitative and a qualitative offering. He gave the firstling of his [entire] flock, and let us not forget it was from over the "process of time." Abel was a herdsman. Sheep can have offspring twice a year, and a typical sheep pregnancy will yield two to three sheep. So if Abel gave the firstling from his flock that means every first sheep was given. Again, we do not know how long "through the process of time" is, but let's just create a number for conversation's sake. Let's say it was 20 years. Sheep are pregnant twice a year, with a minimum of two sheep born each time, and each time Abel would pull the first out and set it aside. Why? It was the "firstling." So 20 years, twice a year, that means he has 40 firstlings set aside.

The text continues to say, "…and the fat thereof." What does that mean? If the first one was bigger than the second one, he didn't try to switch them out so he could keep the bigger one. His willingness to set the first one aside AND to give the fat thereof demonstrates faith to God (Hebrews 11:4). How so?

When it comes time for the offering, Abel brings all 40 sheep and gives them to the Lord and God "has respect to Abel, and to his offering." That's significant. God's attitude towards the giver was impacted by the gift. Why? Because a gift is an extension of the giver's heart and spirit.

Cain gives what he has that day to give. Abel gave what he had been reserving, setting aside, and preparing for God. Do you see the difference? One "did what he could." The other did the best possible. God rejected Cain AND his offering. Again. The gift says something about the heart of the giver. God did not just accept Cain's offering because "at least he gave," or, "at least he's trying." No. God does not function that way. We see Abel practice a principle we later see in the New Testament in Colossians 3:23. "Whatever you do, do it with all of your might."

This attitude that convinces us that God must accept whatever we give in the name of "at least I did this" is an attitude of pride. God is not obligated to accept anything. After all, He is God. Don't conform to the world's standard of honoring God with your life. The "at least" mentality. Why would you aim for the least? Would you aim for the least job? Would you aim for the least pay at that job? Would you aim for the least house or the least car? No. Why aim for the least with God? Give Him your best so that, like Abel, He may have respect to both you and your gift.

Chapter Five

The King's Dominion

In chapter number two we made a bold statement that I promised to come back to. I said that it is possible to be doing what is right and still not bring glory to God. Augustine said, "even the virtues of unbelievers are sin." This is to indict faithless humanistic goodness as contrary and contemptuous towards faith-filled glorification of God.

> **Romans 14:23**
> **But whosoever has doubts is condemned if he eats, because the eating is not from faith. For whatever does not proceed from faith is sin.**

John piper said, "This makes plain that our depravity is a condition in relation to God primarily, and only secondarily in relation to man." You will never really be able to recognize the depth of error that our hearts are naturally bent towards if you assess the heart horizontally rather than vertically. If you measure your goodness from left to right or by measuring against other people (especially those who are not as "God conscious" as you) you will find value in the kind acts that are intrinsic to humanity. It is only when you begin to measure yourself to God, His nature, and His purity that you can properly and completely assess just how defunct our "goodness" is when independent of Him. In one record found in the synoptic gospels (that has been a point of contention amongst those wishing to prove false the deity of Christ), in *Mark 10:17–22*, Jesus says, "No one is good—except God alone."

Jesus was not diminishing His divine self, rather he was glorifying it in pointing out that his goodness was not a result of His humanity but was a direct result of His divinity. An understanding of Hebrews 11:6 is crucial to the life of faith. "***Without faith it is impossible to please God...***" God is not pleased by our humanistic values. Just being a "good person" is not his goal. His pleasure is found in our faith and in our holiness. By holiness I don't mean a particular dress code but existential holiness—that is being totally and completely set apart. Our total confidence and conviction found in Him and in Him alone. When you yield solely to the goodness of your flesh, you are indirectly making your flesh, your desires, your own will your King.

Whatever you obey, follow, and acquiesce to has become your authority. Christ is not only our God; He's become our King. As a native of the Western hemisphere (North America/United States of America) I understand it is often difficult for those of us born into a democratic republic to understand what this verbiage means. Though the word "Kingdom" has become a buzz word, especially in certain church circles, few have grasped an understanding of this gospel.

First, we have to understand that a kingdom is not a religious entity but it is a governmental one. It is a government that is led by a monarch and autonomously governed by that monarch. Specifically, the Kingdom of God is a theocratic monarchy. There are tremendous benefits to being a citizen of a kingdom, and with these great benefits come great responsibilities.

> **Revelation 21:3–4 says** *Now the dwelling of God is with men, and he will live with them. They will be His people, and God Himself will be with them and be their God. He will wipe every tear from their eyes...*

This paints an accurate depiction of God our King's responsibility in our lives as Kingdom citizen. He is responsible for us. He is responsible to walk with us and remain/reside with us. He is responsible to comfort us and, according to Matthew 6, He is responsible to provide for us. "Take no thought for

116

tomorrow" is a bold command. It requires total

dependence and confidence on someone else (God)

taking thought for tomorrow. For many of us such a

measure of vulnerability is frightening and brings

about a sense of discontent.

This is what life in a kingdom is to be like. Your trust is

in your king's ability to fulfill their responsibilities

toward his citizens. Being a "Kingdom citizen" is more

than the latest buzz word or name for the people of

God. It is an acknowledgement of residence and

allegiance. Remember the story of Nabal and Abigail

in 1 Samuel 25? Nabal greatly offended David when

David sent some of his men to request food and

supplies when Nabal not only denied their request but

scoffed at it. The Western democratic mind might say,

"Well, Nabal had a right to say no, it's his stuff."

However, that is a Westerner's way of thinking. In a

kingdom everything the citizens have belongs to the

king. The king is then responsible for the common wealth of his kingdom and to protect everything within it. David had just protected Nabal's properties and the life of his family and he had the nerve to respond to David, the king, in such a way?

When Jesus says, "Take no thought for tomorrow," He's teaching a Kingdom principle. Many of us don't know what that really looks like. Do you remember the carefree almost unconscious life you had as a child? You didn't worry about where food was going to come from; you didn't worry about the lights being paid; you didn't worry about anything. You just woke up, went on about your day, and went to bed. THAT is the freedom that comes with having a King. You are freed from the responsibility of worry. The burdens of concern are lifted off of you because you have a King that is responsible for you, and He is conscious of that responsibility. Some people's childhoods were more challenged than others and I'm sure some might say that the lights didn't turn on every time they flipped the switch. Perhaps you didn't always have as much to eat as you would have liked to. But even in the absence of abundance it was still not your responsibility to worry about it.

As children our principal focus was to please our parents. We didn't want to have to be punished, or disciplined, or have our parents disappointed in us so we learned the art of self-discipline in order to bring joy to the one that was responsible for us; and in turn they rewarded us for our faithfulness in doing what was right under their roof.

> **Psalm 24:1**
> **The earth is the Lord's, and the fulness thereof; the world, and they that dwell therein**

119

At the moment you truly began to fully live out your citizenship you began to relinquish control. You began to realize that nothing belongs to you, which then frees you from the final responsibility of having to worry about all of the details. Everything we have is the King's. WE are the King's. As you begin to rest in this truth you no longer see this is a loss but as a gain.

> **Matthew 16:25**
> **For whosoever will save his life shall lose it: and whosoever will lose his life for my sake shall find it.**

How do you define "life"? Is it your money, your purpose, your success, your family and friends? Perhaps it's the things you've acquired or the power you've amassed. When you place your confidence in those things, when those things begin to diminish or lose value, you've now lost your life. But Jesus says if you release control, whatever you deem to be "life",

He will in return give you true life. In John 10:10 he

reminds us that He came that we might have life in its

fullness. Whether you were born into an affluent

family or in the ghetto, you've not truly begun to

experience life until you know the freedom and joys

that are found in being a Kingdom citizen.

I live stress-free on purpose. It's not accidental or

coincidental. It's not because of how much money I

have, or the house I life in, or the cars that I drive, or

the woman I'm married to. I'm stress-free because

the cares that might otherwise plague me have been

given over to my King. He is responsible for them

now. As I submit myself to His Kingdom I give Him the

legality necessary to then use me for His glory. That

means He has the right to awaken the passion in me

necessary to pursue those things that will advance

His Kingdom. Money, properties, possessions, and seats of power are all things necessary for his authority to be exercised in this realm.

"Realm". What is a realm? It's a word I've heard often in church. "We're going to another realm." But what does that even mean? "Realm" is a Kingdom term so let's break down the anatomy of the Kingdom.

The Kingdom- Though the "Kindom" and "the church" have often been viewed as synonymous they are not. Though they are not the same they are interdependent. "Kingdom" comes from two words —"King" and "Dominion".

The Kingdom then is the King's dominion or the King's domain. It is also His rule being expressed in and through the hearts and lives of those who have submitted to His authority. Those who deny Christ, or refuse His principles, are not a part of His Kingdom.

Realm- A realm is the sphere of influence in which a kingdom has royal domain. It is the king's rule over territories, regions, and systems. It speaks to those areas and places that may not physically be a part of the king's kingdom, but are under his reign. Though these territories may be independent of each other, they share a king. Every realm is identifiable by dimensions. "Dimensions" is another buzz word.

Dimensions- Dimensions are measurements and markers. They say where something starts and where something ends. It is a paradigm of sorts. Like the property you live in has specific dimensions that mark where that property starts and stops. It is containment. It is how one legally identifies rights or how one can identify encroachments. See the image below:

What do those edges do? They contain. The contents within cannot go any further than the dimensions allow. Notice there are 12 edges to this dimension. Twelve is the number of government and order. So then dimensions govern how far one can go. There's not only width and depth in the dimension, there's height. In order to access the heights in the dimension there are various levels or

steps. "Level", another buzz word.

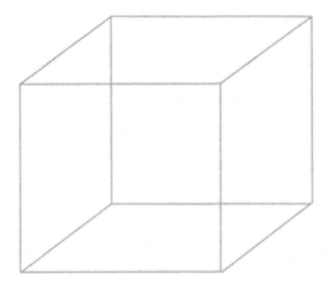

Levels- Levels are flat; however, they position you either above or below one point or the next point. Imagine a hotel with eight floors. Each floor is a level. Say on each floor there are 50 rooms to the right of the elevator and 50 rooms to the left. That means the depth of that floor (or level) is 100 rooms. On floor five you can go to room 550. On floor seven you can go to room 750. Though you may be able to access the same depth on level five that you can on level seven (room 50), you cannot access the same height on level five that you can on level seven. In order to access the next level you need a gate.

Gates- Gates are not only points of entry, but they are points of rule. The gates control access to the levels. Without a gate you can't get to the next level. Be it a door, an elevator, or a fence, every gateway controls access. Every gate can be controlled by keys.

Keys- Keys unlock gateways. They permit the gate to fulfill purpose in being an access point. If the gateway is locked, though the gateway has the potential to grant access, if it's locked it cannot do what it has the potential to do. So keys are important; however, even more important than the key is the locksmith who holds master keys and has the ability to reproduce and grant keys. This is the work of the apostolic ministry gift. We could easily hop down this bunny trail and begin talking about the subject of apostolic ministry, but let's stay on task here.

So you can see that there are many facets to a kingdom, each designed to strengthen and deepen the dominion of that king's domain. I taught a lesson years ago called the "Law of Legal Entry." The lesson is that in order for a king to have authority in a foreign territory he needs to have authority over and in the lives of those who are actually in that territory.

What then does the Kingdom or the King's dominion have to do with Grace? If grace is divine enablement, or divine strength, it is a necessary ingredient to maintaining the King's dominion. How can you maintain His dominion without His strength? If you are to be His agent and His representative you must be endowed with His power. 1 John 4:17 says "...in this world we are as He is." You are as Him in this world.

> **2 Corinthians 5:20**
> **We are therefore Christ's ambassadors, as though God were making His appeal through us...**

"Ambassador" is another governmental term. You are His principle agent. Christ has need of you in order to expand His Kingdom in the earth. At the ends of the ages, according to Revelation 11:15, "the kingdoms of this world" will have "become the kingdoms of our God." That is our assignment. To infiltrate the kingdoms of this world and, through our submission to His nature, allow Him through us to subdue those kingdoms—kingdoms such as banking, real estate, academia, government, media, arts, and family. It is God's will that His people be at the helm of these "kingdoms".

It's virtually impossible to fulfill responsibilities without the necessary authority to do it. If I'm being deployed out of the country and need someone to tend to my business affairs I can't give them that responsibility without giving them the power [of attorney] to fulfill the responsibility. He has given us this major assignment to be "as Him" in the world, to demonstrate His love towards people and to be a beacon of light. That's a difficult thing to do when so many people are not kind in return and when others have done things to hurt us and set us back. How is it possible to be "as Him" when we have so much justification to repay evil for evil?

That is where His grace comes in. Jesus was lied on, spit on, mistreated, rejected, dejected, and misused. Despite all of this He still did what He came to do, which was demonstrate unconditional love towards all who would receive it. He was saddened for those who wouldn't receive it but left the door open for the opportunity for them to later receive it. Can you imagine people literally spitting on you, physically abusing you, rejecting you, yet you still loving them and leaving the door open just in case they change their minds? It was a prime example of their virtues being sin. According to their understanding of the old covenant, and God, they needed to silence this man. Many of them did so without pausing to consider the will of God. Despite all of that the King loved them even more.

Do you have that ability? Consider the worst things that have happened to you in your life. Have you been raped? Abused? Molested? Cheated? Hurt by those closest to you. Rejected by those you loved? Pause and assess how you feel about those people right now. Sure, you may not be wishing any ill against them (and maybe you are), but do you actively love them? Are you able to think greater of them than your own experience with them? I know that sounds like a hard thing to do, and in yourself, in your own "virtues", you probably wouldn't be able to. It is only through His grace (divine ability/strength) that you could do that. And in doing so, it wouldn't be you doing it at all. It would be Him THROUGH you.

Galatians 2:19–20 *For I through the law am dead to the law, that I might live unto God. I am crucified with Christ: nevertheless I live; yet not I, but Christ liveth in me: and the life which I now live in the flesh I live by the* *faith of the Son of God, who loved me, and gave himself for me.*

When you choose to live by the grace of Christ, it ceases to be you living at all. It is HE, the Christ, the one who has taken dominion, He lives no longer you. When you struggle to live the life of unconditional love that Christ has called you to live, it evidences that you are still trying to live as you. When we begin to take on His mind, we begin to pursue His will. As we pursue His will we take on His heart. As we take on His heart those things that seemed too hard for us to do all of a sudden become light and easy! Why? HIS YOKE IS EASY! His burden is light. The weight of the work is no longer before you.

It is only through Christ that true dominion over our existential self is achieved. The Kingdom is again that two-part word; King's - Dominion. It's HIS dominion. You can become a partaker of His dominion through

131

and in His grace. If in fact the cross did what it did do, then through HIS dominion, whatever it is that you are fighting has already been defeated. Why struggle to win a battle that has already been won? Just join the winner's team and become a partaker of His victory.

Chapter Six

Conquering L.U.S.T.

(Living Under Satan's Thumb)

From the end of our previous chapter some might say, "Doc, that's easier said than done." Perhaps you're asking, "How do I live as Christ so that I can receive His strength?" I don't want you to think of this from a natural perspective. Remember the story of Nicodemus in John 3? When he heard Jesus preaching that "we must be born again," he was confused by the notion. Beyond the obvious confusion the true war comes in when you have to take off yourself in order to put on Christ.

Romans 13:14 Rather, clothe yourselves with the Lord Jesus Christ, and do not think about how to gratify the desires of the flesh.

The word translated "clothe" (or put on) is the Greek word "enduo", which means to sink into or to be plunged into. Think about getting on the diving board on the deep end of the pool and jumping into the water. The process of putting on Christ begins by immersing yourselves in Him. How? Like a loved one who's passed away and you later find a notebook of their's; it gives you the opportunity to step into them, their thoughts, their passions and concerns. The word of God is the first foot of water you go through as you dive in. Getting into an environment where every aspect of you can be immersed in the word of God. As the word begins to move through you an internal way will begin. A conflict between what seems to come "naturally" to you and this new way of being. The word of God functions as a detox being introduced into your system. It's designed to make all of the toxins come to the surface. When you make the commitment to putting on Christ, every toxin within you will begin to endeavor to come to the surface, and that's when the true battle begins.

Oftentimes it's in the heat of these battles that we begin to attempt to justify these battles by suggesting God is tempting us. Trying to test us to see what we will do. There are a couple of problems with that line of thinking that I think borderline heresy. First, if God needs us to do what we're going to do in order for Him to know what we're going to do, then He is not omniscient. He should know before anything is done. Secondly, if God both sets up the temptation and then rescues us from it, that's SICK! That would be an extreme case of Munchausen syndrome by proxy. For God to cause us trouble just to rescue us from it makes Him sound much more like a psychopath than a God. Imagine someone setting your house on fire just so that they could come back and rescue you out of the fire. Would you consider that person a hero? Absolutely not!

This is the picture we've allowed ourselves and others to paint of our God. That He tests us just to see what we're going to do. When bad things happen in our lives, we think we give God glory by saying it was the will of God or, worse yet, that God was "in control". There's an entire world of people that are mad at God because of this very line of thinking. Religion has correlated the power of God with the sovereignty of God. Because of this, RELIGION has taught us that God is responsible for everything. God is no more in control of everything than a parent is in control of everything their children do.

I like to use the acronym LUST -

Living Under Satan's Thumb.

Sin is an addiction, and addictions are slave masters. They control what you do, when you do it, and how you do it. They don't care what is damaged, who is hurt, and what casualties are suffered. Through the power of grace you have been FREED from the bondage of sin. You do not have to fall prey to its control anymore. In the United States, President Abraham Lincoln brought an end to slavery by signing the Emancipation Proclamation in 1863. Even though legally all slaves were freed, slaves in the state of Texas did not know that they were free until June 19, 1865. Even after these slaves came to know of their freedom many were deceived into a new type of slavery by a deceptive prison labor system called debt peonage. They got a glimpse and taste of their freedom; then for many it was snatched from them. So first they were free and didn't know it. That's the place many are in even as you read this book. You are already free. Now, learning to live out that liberty is an entirely different conversation.

Imagine having lived your whole life as a slave. Rising at the command of another. Sleeping at the command of another. Being beaten because of the emotions of another. Then, one day, an emancipation proclamation comes. Even though you are freed, bondage and your reaction to bondage has become a habit. As such, you still relate to your freedom from a mentality of bondage. When you relate to freedom from a place of bondage, you wait for the master's permission to be free. Please understand that if slave masters had their way slaves would still be enslaved. Whatever appetite your flesh has waits on the opportunity to re-enslave you.

> **Romans 5:12 NIV**
> **Therefore, just as sin entered the world through one man, and death through sin, and in this way death came to all people, because all sinned—**

David said it best speaking of his own truth in Psalms 51. He said he was born in iniquity and conceived in sin. Because of the fall of the first man, Adam, all of us are born through sinful flesh. We are born with appetites, many of which are learned, developed, and grown from family, relationships, and other patterns we are exposed to. Beyond the natural aspect of our flesh we are spirit beings. So then we war with a second layer of conflict in the human spirit. Things like familiar spirits are real. As mentioned earlier in the book, I don't subscribe to the doctrine of generational curses in the lives of spirit-led believers, but I do believe in generational patterns. Scientifically, habit formation is studied in three phases—cue, behavior, and reward. I call the cue a trigger. It's the thing that triggers or provokes the habit and behavior that comes with the habit. The behavior is the reaction to the trigger. The reward is the feeling or sensation that baits one into the cycle of the habit.

Usually, during the formation of habits those habits go unnoticed. It is not common for someone to pause to assess and analyze himself. It is not until we come into an aspect of enlightened consciousness that we begin to monitor ourselves. Oftentimes, by the time this enlightenment happens we are already in the "habit loop." The more frequently we do things in response to specific other things the more "natural" and automatic the behavior becomes. Scientifically, habits are then written in neurological paths. So now there's a three-dimensional war going on within yourself, and at least at it's unset it is unnoticed. By the time it is noticed, an appetite for the reward has been created and the reward becomes a subconscious goal no matter how detrimental the behavior may be, and no matter how much self-induced damage it may cause, because the reward is now the focus.

It's not until there is a devaluation of both the behavior and the reward that the habit (and subsequent lust) can be interrupted. How often have you paused to consider which spirit gets glory out of your actions? The spirit of God or the spirit of evil? How often do you think from a higher plane than that of your humanity? While living in a realm that is so sensational it is easy to forget that there is indeed an unseen realm, a realm that actively seeks to make use of the decisions of our humanity, whether good or bad. The Kingdom of God looks to the faith-centered discipline of your humanity as an entryway into the earth to both influence and gain legality to govern in and through our lives. In like manner the spirit of darkness looks to the unbridled lasciviousness of our humanity as an entryway into the earth to both influence and gain legality to govern in and through our lives.

The Bible tells a story of the false prophet Balaam who was hired by Balack to bring a curse against the people of God. When he was unable to succeed, his reasoning is found in Numbers.

> **Numbers 23:21**
> **He hath not beheld iniquity in Jacob,**
> **neither hath he seen perverseness in Israel.**
> **The Lord His God is with him, and the shout**
> **of a king is among them.**

No iniquity was beheld, nor was any perverseness seen. There was no legal gateway for the control to be exercised and administrated through. In order for any lust to control you it needs a gateway. Stop. Consider the lusts of your life. What are the gateways that they control through? Is it through certain movies you watch that trigger certain imaginations? Certain people you follow on Instagram? Perhaps it's certain relationships or connections. Remember every spirit needs a gateway. Yes, even the spirit of God. The scripture went on to say that the shout of a king is among them. It's more literally translated that they sound as though they have a King. They didn't sound afraid or vulnerable no matter how exposed they were. They sounded confident that they were well protected.

When you live your life in a way that is dedicated to God, you can be confident that you are well protected. As I've shared before, a king has the responsibility to protect His faithful subjects. He can find security in knowing that His people are His, and His people can find security in knowing that they have a King. Perhaps you are unable to identify just how comforting that is and should be.

Daniel 11:32

...but the people that do know their God shall be strong and do exploits.

See when you know your God, a different level of assurance and confidence comes on you. The kind of confidence that allows you to do phenomenal things, break records, and set new normals. But in order for Him to be our God and King we must be his people. You must be His man or His woman. Your whole heart has to be dedicated to the pursuit of His will for your life. It is only in such a secure and committed relationship that the true grace of God can be released. No it's not that you earn it. It's that you secure it.

This is a most dangerous reality to the kingdom of darkness, the reality that you could actually become a conduit for the grace of God in the earth. In light of this Satan and his legion work overtime to keep you living under Satan's thumb. Pause and consider how difficult it is for you to kick seemingly the simplest habit. Whether it's smoking, drinking, gossiping, overeating, fornication; whatever you lust for, if there is a gateway, that lust is given control over you. It is often easier to blame all of our downfalls on "the will of God", but that is not so.

> **James 1:13–14**
> **Let no man say when he is tempted, I am tempted of God: for God cannot be tempted with evil, neither tempteth he any man: But every man is tempted, when he is drawn away of his own lust, and enticed.**

Temptation comes through the gateway of our own lusts. It is by our own lusts that we are enticed. As such it is only through deliberate government, discipline, and subjection of the flesh that one can begin to live a life free from the control of those things that seek to provide ungodly control in your life. One

146

might feel as though the denial of the appetites that have become so natural to you would be a type of suffering.

> *1 Peter 4:1–2*
>
> *For as much then as Christ hath suffered for us in the flesh, arm yourselves likewise with the same mind: for he that hath suffered in the flesh hath ceased from sin; 2 That he no longer should live the rest of his time in the flesh to the lusts of men but to the will of God.*

The suffering of the flesh leads to the cessation of the life of sin. It is your deliberate choice to subject your own flesh and to deny its appetites that then leads you to a life regulated by the will of God. I know that in cultures governed by sensationalism and sensualities it would seem that a life not governed by them would be impossible. But not so! You can get out from under Satan's thumb. No, you cannot do it by yourself.

However, God cannot do it in your life by Himself either. So often we pray and cry out to God to deliver us; however, the process of self-control is a partnership between God and you. Together you can navigate the uncertain seas of your life's appetites and together you can command them.

I like what the writer of Jude declared in the 24th verse — "Now unto him that is able to keep you from falling..." He CAN keep you. I grew up in church so right there someone would respond, "If you want to be kept."

If it is your desires that have you bound it will take an equal yet opposite desire to free you. As you long for the things of the flesh you can long for the righteousness of God. Just as the longing (lust) of the flesh becomes the gateway for the thing you long for to control you, a longing for the things of God and of faith becomes the gateway for God to regulate your life. It is irresponsible and unrealistic to say, "God, take this from me, and don't let me want it, and let me forget about. Let it not come after me, let them not try to hold on to me..." I once heard a young lady new to pulpit ministry preach this. The church went crazy; however, as I listened I said to myself, "What an irresponsible faith." We want to open the gateways that allow things to bind us but then want God to do all of the work in liberating us. Allow me to be the first to tell you. God will do all of the heavy lifting, but He does require your partnership.

The heavy lifting of those things in life is often the thing that intimidates us from ever beginning the journey (and staying on the journey) of taking total dominion in our life. So then the cowardly way out is to convince yourself that you are in control. "I'm doing this because I want to!" You exclaim. Oh really now?

You're in and out of church because you want to? You get so emotionally overwhelmed that you drown your sorrows in the bottom of a bottle (or two) of wine? You are so in control that your habits have produced distance between you and your children and a sense of self-hate that you then look to your appetites to drown out? No! Be honest with yourself. You want to be free from those things. You desire the serenity of perfect peace. However, it is the "how" that has escaped you. Perhaps for you it is the "how long it will take" that intimidates you. I don't know what agent the enemy has used in you or in your life to keep you under his thumb, but do yourself a favor right now and issue it and him a termination notice.

You will no longer need the services of those distractions. Those things are only useful in the life of those who don't have the strength (or access) to face the day-to-day trials of life head-on. But as the eyes of your understanding are opening there is a confrontational anointing coming onto you. An anointing to confront those things in you that have bound you. An anointing to confront the way of thinking that talks you out of happiness, the way of living that tries to cheat you out of true love and emotional stability. A confrontational anointing to confront the theoretical "thumb" that has held you down.

No! I'm not saying you can do this in and of yourself or by yourself for that matter.

> **Romans 7:18**
> *For I know that in me (that is in my flesh,)*
> *dwells no good thing: for to will is present*
> *with me: but how to perform that which is*
> *good I find not. For the good that I want to*
> *do I do not: but the evil which I don't want*
> *to do, that I do*

I'm sure you can relate to Paul's words in some way.

Perhaps in the past you've made up in your mind to

make some changes but it just got too hard for you.

Maybe you made up your mind to start doing

something like fasting, or praying, or going to church

but didn't get the results you expected. Then you got

discouraged, frustrated, and fell back into the habit

that brought you to bondage in the first place. I would

like to suggest to you that the reason you were

unsuccessful in your pursuit of life changes in the past

is because somewhere along the way you started

trying to do them in your own strength. Somewhere

you started trying to reason your way through them in

your own thinking and it just will not work that way.

While in faith you began to do it your own way, at your

own pace, and that in and of itself is the opposite of

faith. Proverbs says that we shouldn't lean on our

own understanding but that we should trust the Lord

with all of our heart. That means that leaning on your own understanding is the opposite of trusting the Lord with all of your heart.

You cannot do both. Trying to do this on your own might, your own will, your own intellect is a setup for failure. Neither you nor I are that strong. It is only through our faith partnership with God that we can begin to take total victory in our lives. It's through your commitment, but it's based on his strength. It is through your submission, but it is by and through his spirit. A famed passage of scripture says, "It's not by might, nor by power, but by His spirit." That's where the victory is. Not in our might. Remember we are spirit beings so this is a spiritual battle. As long as we are living in this body we (by ourselves) are at a disadvantage. But your faith partnership with God is the advantage. God doesn't have a body to grow tired

153

in. He doesn't have "nerves" to get on the last one of.
He doesn't have feelings to be offended or emotional.
You plus God are an unmatched force to be reckoned
with.

As you learn to lean and depend totally on Him you
may grow weary. Yet at the junction of your weariness
and your faith is His strength. He neither sleeps nor
slumbers! He cannot be distracted, nor can He grow
weary. His grace is inexhaustible!

Chapter Seven

Inexhaustible Grace

Isaiah 40:31 NIV

But those who hope in the Lord will renew their strength. They will soar on wings like eagles; they will run and not grow weary, they will walk and not be faint

In chapter 1 I began to deal with the transposition of grace. Where the popular message of grace has been the freedom to be weak, to give in to the lust of your flesh and to be unconcerned by it, the true message of grace seems like a farce. How is it even possible to soar like eagles, to run and not get weary, and to walk and not be faint? It's possible through the inexhaustible grace of God. When your hope or expectation is in and on God, your strength is renewed daily. Grace is not license to sin. Grace is a license to be strong in a weak world. It is God's strength working through you so that you don't have to depend on your own strength (or weakness). When you are truly in grace, you easily find your way into the Promised Land. What is that? It's what Hebrews 4

talks about.

> **Hebrews 4:1 Let us therefore fear, lest, a**
> **promise being left us of entering into his**
> **rest, any of you**
>
> **should seem to come short of it. 2 For unto**
> **us**
>
> **was the gospel preached, as well as unto**
> **them: but the word preached did not profit**
> **them, not being mixed with faith in them**
> **that heard it.**

The promised place is a place of rest. Not living in

worry, in fear, or overwhelmed by the pressures of life.

Verse 2 tells us how we can find our way into the

Promised Land and how others missed it. It says that

some mixed the word they heard with faith and others

did not. Those that didn't mix the word with faith never

found rest. Those that did inherited it. I closed chapter

1 by saying that the Promised Land of today is not a

geographical one but a place of rest. It's what we find in Hebrews 4. However, Hebrews 4 opens with one of the most freighting realities of faith in my opinion; the reality that it is in fact possible to miss out on God's promises for your life if you don't pursue Him in faith. It is God's desire that you find yourself in a place where the sweat of your brow is a thing of the past. However, His rest is a reward of mixing His word with faith while functioning in His grace. It's not the will of God that you be overworked yet continually under produce. It is His desire that you work easy but produce more than those who work hard.

It is His desire to deliver you from the control of the flesh and from the futile self-righteousness of [false] religion. Is it possible to live in the flesh but not be controlled by it? Yes! Through the divine nature He has made each of us a partaker of.

1 John 3:1 NKJV

Behold what manner of love the Father has bestowed on us, that we should be called the children of God

Tapping into this divine nature is not a work of your own efforts. It is HIS work! We simply have to choose to receive and believe that what He has called us is reflective of who we truly are. He called us His children. Children are a subset of their parents. They are what their parents are, and if God is divine then we are divine. When you try to do it in your own ability, your own holiness, or your own righteousness, you miss it. You make the cross of none effect. His righteousness is replaced by your self-righteousness. Your divine nature is what gives you legality to function in His grace. His grace is divine and it can only be worn by the divine. You must begin to see yourself through the lenses of God. Though you are in a human body you are not that suit of flesh. You are a divine spirit, and through the divine nature you are one with Him. 1 John 4:15–17 says, "Whoever confesses that Jesus is the son of God, God abides in Him and He in God. 16 And we have known and believed the love that God has for us. God is love, and he who abides in love abides in God and God in him. 17 Love has been perfected among us in this: that we may have boldness in the day of judgement: because as He is, so are we in this world."

How can you and I have boldness on the Day of Judgment, the day in which God is looking through "the Lamb's book of life" and judging our works in the worth? None of us have been 100% perfect so how can we have boldness on that day? We can have boldness when we have stepped into Christ and allowed Him to step into us. We have boldness because in Christ we are unseen. The judgment falls upon the one that is perfect and holy.

Verse 17 said, "Even as He is, so are we..." The phrase "even as" is the Greek word "kathos" and it means "exactly as". We are exactly as He is in this world. How is that possible? The law of kinds. If we are his children then what's in Him is in us. Through faith in Christ and baptism in the Lord Jesus you began to take on His image and presence in the world. John 8:12 says that Jesus is the light of the world. But in Matthew 5:13–16 Jesus says we are the light of the world. In verse 2 of 1 John 3 it says when He is revealed, we shall be like Him. "Shall be like" is homoio in Greek, which means the same as Him. Vs. 3 proves it when it says that as He is pure we too will be pure. Understand, however, this is not your purity or righteousness. It is His purity and righteousness. Through the law of imputation He passes is it to us. The grace of Christ allows Christ's strength to come upon you. How? Because it's not really coming upon you it's still on Him and you are now in Him through your faith in Him.

You see grace only works on the man Christ Jesus, and so you must take on that man. You have to bring an end to your own self-centered attempts at righteousness and human virtue.

The entire purpose of the law was to bring an end to our own attempts at righteousness. The law made clear that in man's own attempts there was guaranteed failure at being perfect. The law only has dominion over you as long as YOU live (Romans 7:1).

> **Romans 7:2–3**
> **For the woman who has a husband is bound by the law to her husband as long as he lives. But if the husband dies, she is released from the law of her husband. 3. So then if, while her husband lives, she marries another man, she will be called an adulteress: but if her husband dies, she is**

162

free from the law, so that she is no adulteress, though she is married to another man.

That woman is a type and shadow of us. We (humanity) were married to the law. But through the power of the life of Christ the law was fulfilled allowing the law to be dead to us and we dead to it. As such we have legality to be married (in covenant) with another—that is the Lord Jesus Christ. The writer of Romans acknowledges the war that then begins to wage deep within his soul as His mind seeks to please God but His body finds itself warring to please itself. Have you ever been there? You've put it in your mind to please God, but it seems that your body didn't get the memo. Some have misread the next verse (24) to mean that Paul was hopeless, wondering who could save him. One writer says this in the *Clermont* and some other copies, along with the

Vulgate, read here, χαρις του θεου; the grace of God,

namely, will deliver me. But the common reading,

being supported by almost all the ancient

manuscripts, and the Syriac version, is to be

preferred, especially as it contains an ellipsis, which, if

supplied, according to the apostle's manner, from the

foregoing sentence, will give even a better sense than

the *Clermont* reading, thus: Who will deliver me? I

thank God, who will deliver me, through Jesus Christ.

Thus the apostle beautifully interweaves his

complaints with thanksgiving; the hymn of praise

answering to the voice of sorrow, wretched man that I

am! So then he here sums up the whole and

concludes what he had begun. We've got to consider

verse 24–25 against the backdrop of Romans 6:8.

"Now if we died with Christ, we believe that we

shall also live with Him." And we can't stop there,

we have to read Romans 5:6 "For when we were still

without strength, in due time Christ died for the ungodly." It makes it plain that Paul in Chapter 7 is not glorifying the power of sin in his life. But he is diminishing its power in light of his covenant with Christ. "WHO SHALL DELIVER ME"; then He answers himself, "THE LORD JESUS CHRIST!" See your deliverance is in Christ and your total dependence on Him.

Again, grace is the end of you and the beginning of Christ in you. It's a clear line of demarcation. Romans 1:17 says that the righteousness of God is revealed from faith to faith. However, it is more literally translated, "the righteousness *that proceeds from God...*" No, it's not your own righteousness or a merit of your work. It is the righteousness that is imputed to you as you enter the Kingdom of God. Through the grace of Christ you become righteous. A life of sin is then beneath your station in the Kingdom. You have a

noble obligation to live up to the righteousness of the

crown of glory that has been placed on your head.

Through the grace of Christ you daily cease to be the

man or woman you were. 2 Corinthians 5:17 says that

if any man be in Christ he is a new creature and old

things are passed away. As you are reading this you

are reading the eulogy of your old man. The cause of

death? The grace of Christ!

> **Titus 2:11–12**
> **For the grace of God that brings salvation**
> **has appeared to all men, 12 teaching us**
> **that, denying ungodliness and worldly lusts**
> **we should live soberly, righteously, and**
> **godly in the present age.**

Does that sound like the grace you've heard

preached, the grace that says, "Don't worry about

your fleshly struggles because grace has you

covered"? The [false] doctrine of grace that says,

"Don't feel any type of way about it, God knows your heart"? NO! The grace of God brings salvation! His grace enables you to deny ungodliness and worldly lusts. His grace teaches and enables you to live soberly, righteously, and godly IN THE PRESENT AGE. Does that sound like this weak message of grace that has been made so popular? NO! Grace is power, not weakness. It's strength. Divine strength. It's the power to say no when everyone else is saying yes. It's the power to deny your flesh, not to give into it and accept it. Galatians 5:1 already told us that sin is bondage. Let's look at it again.

Galatians 5:1
Stand fast therefore in the liberty wherewith Christ hath made us free, and be not entangled again with the yoke of bondage.

What did He make us free from? Romans 8:2 said he set us free from the law of sin and death. So SIN is that bondage. Sin is not freedom. Yet, the false message of grace says you're free to sin because grace has you covered. Consistently falling into the lusts of your flesh is not being free. That, my friend, is being bound. And I know some say, "Well, why won't God just take these desires away from me?"

Vs. 2 answers that question when Paul says, "If ye be circumcised, Christ shall profit you nothing." What does circumcision do? It removes the excess flesh. Paul says if all of the excess flesh is removed God gets no glory. If God has to take it all away from you in order for you to have power over it, He gets no glory. He gets glory when you still have the potential and the proclivity to do those old things but you're so immersed in grace that you choose not to. THAT brings God glory. Some things he leaves with you. It keeps you dependent on His grace knowing that you only have power over it through him.

Whatever the proclivity of your flesh is, you do not have to be a slave to it. Homosexuality, fornication, adultery, and the list goes on... You do not have to be its slave.

> **2 Kings 5:1**
> **Now Naaman, captain of the host of the king of Syria, was a great man with his master, and honourable, because by him the LORD had given deliverance unto Syria: he was also a mighty man in valour, but he was a leper.**

This text poses a cultural conflict. This man is called a great man, honorable, and a mighty man of valor. But it also says he was a leper. How is that possible? Culturally a leper was excommunicated from society. They were not considered honorable or great, but they were considered as cursed. Lepers were put out of the city and definitely couldn't come into the presence of nobility, so how is this man given all of these accolades yet is a leper? Well, it's obvious to me. He had an issue (leprosy) but didn't live it out. He didn't live like his issue. Whatever your "issue" is, you do not have to live it out. Leprosy was not a surface issue, though it manifested itself in external ways, like skin turning white. Just like whatever your issue is. What you see is the manifestation, but it's not the root issue. Homosexuality is not the issue. That's just the manifestation. Fornication is not the issue. That's just the surface manifestation. The issue is deep beneath the surface deposited in the "city of your soul." Though your issue may absolutely be present its presence doesn't necessitate a manifestation. You do not have to choose to allow it to administrate itself throughout your life. But the greater issue is when your issue is not submerged and surrounded in grace.

I remember watching one of the *X-men* movies and the character "Magneto" had such a great supernatural power that they locked him into a tank-like enclosure to disengage the strength of what had become an issue. Grace is that tank. It can disengage the strength of your issue if you submerge yourself in it. Yes, there are indeed some things that you won't be able to circumcise. You will live with them your entire life. But they don't have to live through you. Don't lend your body, your mind, and your heart to their use. If allowed, the enemy will manipulate and exploit your weaknesses as tools for your demise. The path of least resistance is to convince yourself that what you know is ungodly is in fact Godly. It's what our society encourages us to do. We're encouraged to redefine things and to force definitions that contradict true meanings.

Deep within each of us, however, is a still small voice. A voice that pricks our hearts, stirs in our souls, and attempts to charge our spirit. This voice is God's voice. No matter how deep the struggle, or how deep-seated the issue His still small voice is there. He made us a promise never to leave us and never to forsake us. This is a new covenant promise. Though He will never leave us the question you have to ask yourself is "Is that enough?" Is His capacity to look beyond and over our faults enough?

At some point, as you begin to mature and divorce your selfish nature, you don't just want Him with you; you want Him pleased with you. Right? Think about it in the natural. Would you want your spouse to be with you out of obligation to their own commitment? No good person would. You want your spouse to honor their commitments, but because of your love for them you want to be pleasing to them so that honoring those commitments is something of joy in their life.

This is the heart's cry of any person who truly

understands the value of a loving God and the value

of being able to make full use of His grace. Your heart

is to please Him. But we know that in our own

capacity we will constantly fail Him. As a matter of

fact, attempting to do it in and on our own capacity is

in itself a slap in the face of God. Not only is God's

grace available to you, but He wants you to make full

use of it.

> **Isaiah 30:18**
> **Yet the LORD longs to be gracious to you;**
> **therefore he will rise up to show you**
> **compassion. For the LORD is a God of**
> **justice. Blessed are all who wait for him!**

Do you see that? He passionately desires to extend

His grace to you. Though we are raised to be self-

sufficient, and subsequently self-serving, He still

desires to extend His grace and compassion to you. He considers it justice to extend that grace to you! How could it be justice? After all, none of us are worthy, right? Well, yes and no! We ourselves are not worthy; however, our sin nature is a product of the fall of Adam. None of us asked to be born with whatever fleshly proclivity we may have. So in redeeming mankind it is justice in the mind of God to give you the capacity to control the thing that has attempted to control you your whole life. Why? It's not your fault.

Allow me to free you. The root cause of your issues, be it mental, emotional, sexual or spiritual, is not your fault. As such, God has given you His grace to be the advantage over those things. Now, although the root cause is not your fault, choosing to allow it to live out in your life is your choice.

Though you may grow weary fighting within yourself His grace is Inexhaustible. It never runs out. The entirety of Psalm 136 is dedicated to reminding us that God's love never fails. When you feel as though you have failed, as though you have slipped into your own understanding and in doing so have disappointed God, simply remind yourself, "His love never fails." His grace never weakens.

Isaiah 26:4
Trust ye in the Lord for ever; for in the LORD JEHOVAH is everlasting strength

Trust ye in THE LORD! Remember, anytime you read "The Lord" (or what the NIV often translates as sovereign God) that gives reference to God not as a deity but as Ruler. The one in charge and seated on the throne. If your fate or mine was left to the hands of earthly justice or even fairness we would all be cast away. Thanks be to God that His system does not

175

work like ours. He does not give us what is fair. He gives us what is just, and because He is the Lord it is He that determines what is just. Psalm 46:1 says that, "God is our refuge and strength, a very present help in trouble." You can hide yourself in God's grace and strength. Your weakness never has to take the center stage of your life when the grace of God is where your life is submitted. His strength is illuminated in the midst of your weakness. So it is not weakness that steals the spotlight. Your weakness becomes a very faint backdrop. His strength is what shines, and your weakness's only claim to fame is that it provided a spotlight for the strength of God to shine through.

You see light is brightest in a dark room, and strength is seen the strongest in the midst of weakness. If you walk into a gym full of physically fit, buff, strong men, then men lifting bars full of heavy weight don't stand out. But if you walk into a gym of average and less than average people in terms of their physical fitness

but there's one physically fit, buff, strong man in the

back lifting a bar full of heavy weight that man stands

out! Why? Because he's surrounded by weakness.

Your weakness is nothing to be ashamed of. Guilt and

condemnation can only rule your life when you allow

your weakness to rule your life.

> *2 Corinthians 12:*
> *8 For this thing I besought the Lord thrice, that*
>
> *it might depart from me.(And he said unto me,*
>
> *My grace is sufficient for thee: for my strength is made perfect in weakness. Most gladly therefore will I rather glory in my infirmities, that the power of Christ may rest upon me. 10 Therefore*
>
> *I take pleasure in infirmities, in reproaches, in necessities, in persecutions, in*

distresses for Christ's sake: for when I am
weak, then am I strong.

Paul said he can glory in his infirmities (weaknesses)

because those weaknesses give way to the power of

God. Right when his weakness attempts to overtake

him he looks to Jesus for grace and then his truth

takes a change. His truth was "I am weak." But by the

grace of God, when he is weak, his new truth is "I am

strong." The grace of God has the power to give you a

new truth. It has the ability to alter the truth of your

flesh in order to expose the truth of the grace of Christ

in your life. The message of cheap grace diminishes

the truth of the grace of Christ in our lives and makes

our prerogative to be flawed the spotlight. That's

backwards! Paul says that his weakness being

controlled by the strength of Christ is part of what

evidences his apostolic ministry. The stronger your

call in God the stronger your weaknesses will seem to

178

be. But the deeper in grace you go the weaker your weaknesses become.

As you read this I speak a second wind come over you. Breathe deeply and receive the grace of God into your heart. All that you have been carrying carry no longer! Growing tired is the evidence that you have been carrying all the weight. The only way you can run and not grow weary is if you learn to use His legs. It's not that you no longer have your usual load; it's that he is carrying the weight of the load. Your part is to simply take his yoke upon you. A yoke was used to keep two beasts together headed in the same direction. The Bible says that in order to walk into this easy stress-free reality you do have to take on the yoke of Christ. That means you can't do it your own way. You can't go your own direction. You don't get to move at your own pace. You have to stay in sync with who you are yoked up with.

Read these prophetic words to yourself. "Where you are tired, where you struggle, and where you've been defeated: you will be tired no more! You will struggle no more! You are not defeated! His grace is my advantage, and His grace is inexhaustible!"

Chapter Eight

Mercy & Forgiveness

One of the enemy's principal weapons used to try to prohibit you from making full use of grace in your life is condemnation. The word "condemnation" is a legal one. It refers to charges bring brought against a perpetrator after a crime is discovered or the legal liability of punishment for a crime. Finally, condemnation is a verdict of judgment. The spirit of condemnation is in direct conflict with the grace of God in that condemnation weakens freedom. But greater than it's conflict with grace is its conflict with mercy.

Many confuse grace with mercy or use the words interchangeably as though they are synonyms. Grace is divine strength. Mercy is kindness, generosity, and compassion. The English dictionary defines it as,

"compassion or forgiveness shown towards

someone who it is within one's power to punish or harm."

> *Ephesians 2:4–6*
> *But God who is rich in mercy, for His great love wherewith he loved us, 5 Even when we were dead in sins, hath quickened us together with Christ, by grace are ye saved; 6 And hath raised us up together, and made us sit together in heavenly places in Christ Jesus.*

The word mercy in the above scripture is the Hebrew word "eleos". It means good will towards the miserable and the afflicted joined with a desire to help them. The Bible says that God is rich in this desire because of His abundance of love for us. He's so rich in this desire that even when we were still bound and dead in sin He gave us the grace (divine strength) necessary to find our way to His mercy. The availability of the mercy of God is what the enemy works over time to try to keep you from becoming consciously aware of. If he can keep you bound to the devalued sense of self-worth that sin and shame produces he knows you'll not take advantage of the mercy of God. You'll feel so unworthy of it that you'll convince yourself it's impossible for God to look past all of your past. The sole intent of condemnation is to bring focus to the infraction.

It's designed to keep you focused on what you did, how dumb you were for doing it, and how disappointed God must be in you. Through the same door that these thoughts come in through your peace exits.

> *Isaiah 26:4*
> *You will keep him in perfect peace all who trust in you, all whose thoughts are fixed on you (NLT)*

You see, if he can get your thoughts focused on what you did then he's gotten your mind unfocused from Christ. You can't be 100% focused on two things at the same time. Focusing on one displaces the other. His ultimate goal is to get you out of the rest and contentment that abiding in the grace of Christ provides. He wants to cheat you of the perfect peace that Christ-centered abiding faith allows you to take advantage of. You must become consciously aware of the enemy's desire to manipulate and use the realities of your past as darts against your present. According to Ephesians 6:16, it is only the shield of faith that can quench the fiery darts of the evil one. What is faith? Total confidence, right? So if he can break your confidence in God's love for you and in His ability to redeem you he subsequently lowers your shield, exposing you to his darts.

In order for there to be condemnation there has to be an accusation. Accusation is the work of an accuser; however, they can only affect your life according to the degree of attention and belief you give them.

> **Revelation 12:10**
> **And I heard a loud voice saying in heaven, Now is come salvation, and strength, and the kingdom of our God, and the power of his Christ; for the accuser of our brethren is cast down, which accused them before our God day and night.**

Satan lodges daily accusations against you because he fears that great day. The day when the power of our Christ casts down into the abominable abyss is his worst nightmare. As such, it is his pursuit to ensure as many of us are included in that place with him. He is in fact the enemy of our soul; yet he uses the soul as a toolbox for his assault against our spirit's right standing with God. The soul being the seat of emotions, desires, will, and appetite; what greater resource from which to pull darts from to launch against us? The accusations in and of themselves are not what makes him our enemy. It is the intent, goal, purpose, and object of his accusations that mark him as our enemy. If he were to bring the accusation in order to provoke restoration it would identify him as a true friend.

I remember once a friend of mine spiraling down in the emotions of life. When he found refuge in alcohol, I confronted him and accused him of his works. However, my intent is what made me his friend. Satan's intent is to vex us, harass us, and, above all, to embarrass Christ in us.

The law brought accusation against us, but the law was not our enemy. The law was a school master with the assignment to bring us to Christ and to awaken the realization that in and of ourselves there was no righteousness. Satan, however, uses accusations to drive us back within ourselves. He wants us dependent on self in that he knows our own works can never sustain us. He is not a stupid accuser at all, however. He mixes just enough truth in with his accusations to make the line of thinking that stems from those accusations seem to be a justifiable thought process. It would be justifiable that you be unredeemable if God had not thrown the record of your sins into "the sea of forgetfulness"; the scripture says he will forgive our wickedness and remember our sins no more in Hebrews 8:12. It's justifiable to think you are unlovable if in fact you are just the sum total of the failures of your past. Of course God is "waiting to catch you with your works undone." All of these thoughts stem from the enemy's own self-hate.

It's easy to paint everyone else as hateful when you are the essence of hate.

> **John 12:47**
> **And if any man hear my words, and believe not, I judge him not: for I came not to judge the world, but to save the world.**

Christ said He came to save the world, not to condemn it. Much like a thief, condemnation will often put on masks in order to put the blame on the face of the mask rather than the identity of the actual perpetrator. Condemnation often masks itself as conviction in order to provoke you to have offense with conviction. It is in this spirit that the whole "you can't judge me" paradigm has taken over our culture. Condemnation works to desensitize us to conviction because it is conviction that draws us back to Christ. Conviction is a work of the Holy Spirit. It is designed to produce a God consciousness and a Christ-

centeredness. Godly conviction manifests in times of
Godly sorrow.

> **2 Corinthians 7:10**
> **Godly sorrow brings repentance that leads
> to salvation,and leaves no regret. but
> worldly sorrow brings death.**

Condemnation works to take on the mask of
conviction so that you say to yourself, "No, I'm not
going to allow myself to think about this or feel this
way; it is what it is." Condemnation is a sorry that
leads to death. Conviction is a sorrow that leads to
repentance. The word repentance is the Greek word
"metanoia", which means a change of mind or to
reconsider. Repentance is not just words that you say.
"God forgive me." NO! That is watered-down
repentance that comes out of the message of false
grace. True repentance means to reconsider. It
means that you've confronted yourself and your

190

thinking and have committed to a change. This is what conviction is designed to do. Conviction brings your focus back to Christ and should stir within you a sense of responsibility to His Kingdom. It will remind you, "You've got a call; you've got work to do; the Kingdom needs you. You need to be at church."

And then condemnation will try to overtake conviction and say, "You're worthless; you better not show your face at church they'll all be staring at you, you're such a disappointment." Whichever spirit (conviction or condemnation) you give your ear to you give your heart over to.

How do you identify the difference between the voice of conviction and the voice of condemnation? Condemnation tells you that you are a failure. It interrogates you and asks you, "Why are you so dumb? How could you do that?" It badgers you and says, "You deserve to be miserable, don't you? You got what you deserved; it's all your fault."

Conviction, however, says, "No, you made some wrong choices, but it's not too late to learn principles to master the right choices."

Condemnation produces a pretentious arrogance and is often evidenced in self-righteous defense. "I don't need anybody to tell me what I did wrong. God knows my heart. I don't need anybody in my business." Because condemnation is a work of darkness it influences you to keep your challenges in the dark. You begin to find comfort in relating to the dysfunctions of your life rather than conquering them. You may tell what you do, but not to get help; you'll tell what you do in the attitude of, "I ain't got nothing to hide; I don't care what anyone thinks about me." Then condemnation steals your voice and keeps you from shining light on what has been at work in your life. Why? Because a force of darkness (which is what condemnation is) only has power in darkness.

Conviction, however, runs you to Jesus. It awakens the spirit of humility provoking you to confess your faults knowing that he is faithful and just to forgive you; that he is willing to cleanse you of all unrighteousness (1 John 1:9). Conviction produces humility and it drives your focus up to the goodness of God. It makes you humbled at the thought that, despite the many accusations that had been lodged against you, He still justified you and wants to be gracious towards you.

> **Isaiah 30:18**
> **Therefore the Lord longs to be gracious to you, and therefore he waits on high to have compassion on you.**

Do you see the difference? Condemnation tries to drive your head down in guilt and shame. Conviction lifts your head up to look towards Christ and to think on the things that are above. Remember Philippians 4:8 says that those things that are true, honest, just, pure, lovely, and of good report; your praise will come from thinking on those things. No wonder the enemy works overtime to keep you focused on negative things. If allowed, the work of condemnation will neutralize the power of grace in your life and silence the voice of mercy in your hearing. Condemnation will force you back into your own works, your own righteousness, thus making the cross of none effect in your life.

In order to fully embrace the work of conviction, however, you must truly believe that the end result is what God in fact wants. Conviction drives you back to

Christ. You've got to settle in your heart that no matter what your past has been God still desires you.

You cannot understand the fullness of such an unconditional love through your natural human reasoning. After all, the reality is most of us greatly struggle to love like that if truth be told. We say things like, "I can forgive you, but I can't forget." We'll forgive people but we don't want to reconcile with them, and because we experience God and the love of Christ through our humanity we try to fit Him within our human reasoning. God is much different than we are, however. He loves you and never stops loving you. When you mess up and finally come to yourself, He not only forgives you but He accepts you as though you never messed up. That's God's mercy at work.

Understanding the mercy of God is necessary in order to fully receive the work of grace in your life. Mercy is God's intentional compassion towards man. It's not a compassion based on feelings, its compassion based solely on His will to be compassionate towards us. God's mercy towards us is reinforced by our convictions towards Him.

The principal Hebrew word for our English word mercy is "hesed". This word means "God's covenant lovingkindness." As new covenant believers God has committed and promised Himself to be merciful toward us. As such, mercy is foundational of the new covenant.

David understood the manifest mercies of God so much so that he dedicated the whole of Psalm 136 to talking about it. Do me a favor. Don't skim or skip over this. I want you to read **Psalm 136**. Here it is:

1 O give thanks unto the Lord; for he is good: for his mercy endureth for ever. 2 O give thanks unto the God of gods: for his mercy endureth for ever. 3 O give thanks to the Lord of lords: for his mercy endureth for ever. 4 To him who alone doeth great wonders: for his mercy endureth for ever. 5 To him that by wisdom made the heavens: for his mercy endureth for ever. 6 To him that stretched out the earth above the waters: for his mercy endureth for ever. 7 To him that made great lights: for his mercy endureth for ever 8 The sun to rule by day: for his mercy endureth for ever 9 The moon and stars to rule by night: for his mercy endureth for ever. 10 To him that smote Egypt in their firstborn: for his mercy endureth for ever:

11 And brought out Israel from among them: for his mercy endureth for ever: 12 With a strong hand, and with a stretched out arm: for his mercy endureth for ever. 13 To him which divided the Red sea into parts: for his mercy endureth for ever: 14

And made Israel to pass through the midst of it: for his mercy endureth for ever: 15 But overthrew Pharaoh and his host in the Red sea: for his mercy endureth for ever. 16 To him which led his people through the wilderness: for his mercy endureth for ever. 17 To him which smote great kings: for his mercy endureth for ever: 18 And slew famous kings: for his mercy endureth for ever: 19 Sihon king of the Amorites: for his mercy endureth for ever: 20 And Og the king of Bashan: for his mercy endureth for ever:21 And gave their land for an heritage: for his mercy endureth for ever: 22 Even an heritage unto Israel his servant: for his mercy endureth for ever. 23 Who remembered us in our low estate: for his mercy endureth for ever: 24 And hath redeemed us from our enemies: for his mercy endureth for ever. 25 Who giveth food to all flesh: for his mercy endureth for ever. 26 O give thanks unto the God of heaven: for his mercy endureth for ever.

David takes the time to make clear the mercies of God by juxtaposing them to the state of depravity of humanity. Mercy is existentially woven within the very nature of God. It is part of what makes Him holy and what makes Him sovereign. His choice to be merciful independent of our ability to deserve mercy sets Him in a class all by Himself. The work of the cross and the redemption of Christ is the clearest and strongest demonstration of God's mercy. He was beaten, lied on, spit on, and misunderstood. The same people He deliberately came for rejected Him. Despite all of this, He still chose to die so that we could live. He knew that in our impoverished human state we couldn't be like him, but that was unacceptable to Him. So He became like us so we could still be like Him. That's love on steroids.

2 Corinthians 8:9
For you know the grace of our Lord Jesus

Christ, that though he was rich, yet for your sake he became poor, so that you through his poverty might become rich.

This is not materialistic poverty. The opulence of heaven is not sourced by the material riches of the earth. The riches that He left were the wealth of the attributes of His divine nature. He laid down his rights to demonstrate and live out His divinity and became poor. How? By taking on human flesh. He bankrupted His ability to stretch out in His divine nature so that we could have a pattern for how to take supernatural dominion while in our human bodies. He ensured we didn't have to play a guessing game or a game of trial and error with our lives.

Why do we insist on having to try everything ourselves? Wisdom tells us to learn from the experience of others and to maximize the benefits of their experiences. This is a type of generational wealth. Scripture says He bankrupted Himself to transfer that wealth to you and me. The challenge is, however, that many of us cannot fully understand why a God so rich would want to exchange places with us, born so poor. That is a degree of mercy that the common mind cannot fathom. That is a kind of mercy that you might perhaps struggle to afford to someone else.

Truth be told, the reason many struggle with receiving the mercy and forgiveness of God is because we struggle to extend that kind of mercy and forgiveness to others. To fully begin to walk in mercy and forgiveness you must fully understand your debt.

Romans 5:8
But God demonstrates his own love for us in this: while we were still sinners Christ died for us.

2 Corinthians 5:21

201

God made him who had no sin to be sin for us, so that in him we might become the righteousness of God.

The price of your justification with God is the life of Christ Jesus. That's how valuable He found you to be, valuable enough to become man; valuable enough to suffer [for you] as a man; and valuable enough to die for you. Your debt was so great that it could only be satisfied by blood, the blood of an unblemished sacrifice. This was the God-man Christ Jesus. Perfectly divine, and perfectly human. Perfect enough to satisfy your debt and to make you righteous. Despite all of your hang-ups, mess-ups, and idiosyncrasies, you [through Christ] are now righteous! The most humbling part is that you did not deserve it, and you couldn't earn it, and you still can't afford it. But He affords it to you anyway. How could anyone not humbly devote their life to a God like that?

202

It is not until you fully embrace and acknowledge the work of mercy in your own life that you will really begin to be the merciful person God wants you to be in others' lives. Matthew 5:7 says blessed are the merciful: for they shall obtain mercy. Merciless people are often those who have forgotten the extensive amount of mercy that they daily receive from the Lord.

> *Matthew 18*
>
> *21 Then came Peter to him, and said, Lord, how oft shall my brother sin against me, and I forgive him? till seven times? 22 Jesus saith unto him, I say not unto thee, Until seven times: but, Until seventy times seven. 23 Therefore is the kingdom of heaven likened unto a certain king, which would take account of his servants. 24 And when he had begun to reckon, one was brought unto him, which owed him ten thousand talents. 25 But forasmuch as he had not to pay, his lord commanded him to be sold, and his wife, and children, and all*

that he had, and payment to be made. 26 The servant therefore fell down, and worshipped him, saying, Lord, have patience with me, and I will pay thee all.

27 Then the lord of that servant was moved with compassion, and loosed him, and forgave him the debt. 28 But the same servant went out, and found one of his fellowservants, which owed him an hundred pence: and he laid hands on him, and took him by the throat, saying, Pay me that thou owest. 29 And his fellowservant fell down at his feet, and besought him, saying, Have patience with me, and I will pay thee all. 30 And he would not: but went and cast him into prison, till he should pay the debt. 31 So when his fellowservants saw what was done, they were very sorry, and came and told unto their lord all that was done. 32 Then his lord, after that he had called him, said unto him, O thou wicked servant, I forgave thee all that debt, because thou desiredst me: 33 Shouldest not thou also

*have had compassion on thy fellowservant,
even as I had pity on thee? 34 And his lord
was wroth, and delivered him to*

*the tormentors, till he should pay all that
was due unto him.35 So likewise shall my
heavenly Father do also unto you, if ye from
your hearts forgive not every one his
brother their trespasses.*

Have you ever found yourself being this servant? The
servant who is unforgiving, holds grudges, and feels
justified in doing so? Whether in your day-to-day life
or in what you might consider major situations is the
work of mercy flowing through you or have you
become a dam, receiving mercy but allowing it to stop
in you and not emitting it to others? Maybe someone
lied on you, cheated on you, raped you, stole from
you, or stabbed you in the back. Perhaps you were
given up for adoption at birth or were treated as the
black sheep of the family? Maybe you experience the

daily plights of being born a minority and you hold it against every person who is not a part of your minority group. Is their debt to you greater than your debt was (and still is) to Christ? Is the apology, restitution, or reparations you feel owed greater than what you owe to Christ? Perhaps you feel like you've forgiven too many times and feel like your life is just a doormat. How many times has the Lord had to forgive you, not over the course of your life but just today? The faithless thinking, the carnal living, and the like are all justifiable reasons for Him to disconnect from you, but He doesn't. Because mercy and forgiveness is an innate part of His nature he can't help but extend it to you.

The next time you feel justified in holding a grudge pause to remember what free mercy you have received. Choose to extend it as readily as you receive it. Mercy and forgiveness are a large part of what draws people to Christ. If you are going to be His representative you will have to learn to master this major aspect of His nature.

John 13:35 says By this shall all men know that ye are my disciples; the love you have shown one to another. It is not your spiritual gift, wisdom, and power that makes your relationship with Christ most evident. It is the love of Christ working through you that makes it most evident and testifies of His truth. The value of mercy in your life can be determined by what it is able to purchase. In your life and in mine it has purchased our righteousness.

Righteousness is the only way that we can gain eternal life; so then the value of mercy is eternal life. Since you cannot work for it and it is extended freely we are found eternally in the debt of the mercy of

Christ. How is that debt paid? It is paid through love and through love that is given to His people.

As Kingdom ambassadors we must be the principal examples of love, mercy, and forgiveness. Not the kind of false forgiveness that says, "I forgive but I don't forget," but the kind of love that says, "I don't consider the debt anymore." The kind of love that says, "He paid my debt in full even before I knew to ask for it, so I'm going to cancel your debt in full (forgive) even if you don't ask for it." The greater the level of love, mercy, and forgiveness you walk in the greater the ambassador of Christ you become. He increases the territory of your ambassadorship as you increase in love and mercy.

I know that true forgiveness is hard, especially when you think of how wrong that person was. But it becomes easier the clearer you become about how wrong you have been. Focusing on the wrong cannot

be the end thought, however; that will lead to guilt and

shame. You must see your wrong but allow the mercy

of Christ to be the backdrop of that thought. That way

of thinking will produce Godly conviction. I know you

may be saying, "Now, this sounds good, but how in

the world can I really forget what they did to me?" It's

not so much about forgetting as it is about not

considering.

In Hebrews 8:12 it quotes, "FOR I WILL BE

MERCIFUL TO THEIR INIQUITIES, AND I WILL

REMEMBER THEIR SINS NO MORE." Mercifulness

is found in our capacity to "remember their sins no

more." The word "remember" in Greek is "mimnesko."

It means to be "mindful of." It's not that you have

amnesia; it's simply that this is not where you allow

your thoughts to rest. Remember *Philippians 4:8:*

"Finally, brethren, whatsoever things are true, whatsoever things are honest, whatsoever things are just, whatsoever things are pure, whatsoever things are lovely, whatsoever things are of good report; if there be any virtue, and if there be any praise, think on these things." NO! Don't be mindful of what they did or didn't do to or for you. Be mindful of those things that call you to a higher level of consciousness and existence.

There are people who live dead because they've allowed the offenses they have suffered to suffocate the work of mercy in their life. Doing so bankrupts the divine wealth [nature] that Jesus gave to us. You can't both be godly and bitter. You can't be both godly and unforgiving. One cancels out the other. When you really begin to understand what it means to be an ambassador, you understand that your actions are not independent representations of yourself anyway.

Everything you do, you do on behalf of the King you

represent. It then becomes easy to give mercy

because there's more where that came from! It's not

your mercy anyway! GIVE IT AWAY. Become known

as a merciful man or woman. Make it your goal to

have that be something that people remember about

you. When pride starts saying, "You're a doormat,

they're taking advantage of you, etc.," pull on the

spirit of humility. Remind yourself that you daily take

advantage of the mercy of God. To be clear, I'm not

saying allow people to abuse you or misuse you. I'm

saying if they do, forgive them. There is no freer

person than the one who has freed those persons

who have wronged you. Walk in that freedom.

When you are an ambassador, not only does

everything you do reflect on the King you represent,

but everything that is done to you is not done to you

but to the King. You don't ever have to feel the need to vindicate yourself when you realize who you are to God. He's got you covered.

Chapter Nine

Not a Sinner Saved by Grace

Jesus said in Matthew 7 that we would be able to identify a tree by the fruit that it bears. Before defecting into the Kingdom of God, as outsiders we are without defense before God. Our lives, our fleshly works, and our wicked hearts qualify us for eternal damnation standing before God without justification or defense before God.

> *Much more then, having now been justified by His blood, we shall be saved from wrath through Him. For if when we were enemies we were reconciled to God through the death of His Son, much more, having been reconciled, we shall be saved by His life —* Romans 5:9-10

Justification is a central theme to the gospel of Jesus Christ. Throughout the Book of Romans Paul paints the clear picture of our sinful nature that is hopeless without the help of Christ. He shows us that it is not our works that save us but what God has done as

Christ in the earth that saves us. It is important that we understand the cause and effect that is at work. Your commitment to God is not what makes you right with God. Your realization that Christ has placed you in right standing with God is what provokes the righteous heart to commit to God. The work of Christ is the cause. Commitment, works, holiness is the effect. Your conviction in Christ alters your works. Your works don't produce your standing in Christ. At the moment you accept the work of Christ you are covered, redeemed, and saved. Not by yourself but through and in Christ. 2 Corinthians 5:17 says if any man be in Christ he is a new creature. It is Christ that is truly righteous, and He extends His righteousness as an umbrella to all that are in Him.

The justification of Christ removes the penalty of your sinful nature. Your sinful works before Christ no longer have a voice in the courtroom of heaven against you.

The atoning sacrifice of Christ declares you holy and righteous. Justification is a legal term. The legal dictionary defines it as a "legal excuse for the performance or non-performance of a particular act as that is the basis for exemption from guilt." Christ loved and loves you so much that He chooses not to stand with you. No! He stands AS you. He stands in your place. It is not you that God considers; it is Christ that He considers. You are no longer who or what you were. His truth becomes your truth. You are no longer considered separately from Christ. You are considered through Christ.

One of the most offensive things you can do is disregard a costly gift that someone gave you without cause. Let's say someone takes their life savings and buys you a car, but you refuse to drive it and you tell people, "I still have to walk everywhere I go." Perhaps you have kidney failure and someone decides to give

216

you a kidney. After you've received the kidney they overhear you telling people, "I'm on the transplant list. I could die any day now." Maybe you have children and you work two or three jobs to provide for them but you overhear them saying, "I wish I could have just a few things I like. Mom and Dad never get us anything!" You would be hurt, offended, and feel disrespected, right? It would probably feel like you've been taken for granted and that your efforts have gone unnoticed.

Oftentimes, in an attempt to honor God, we actually dishonor Him and His work for our lives. We identify ourselves in ways that diminish the finished work of Christ, the work that our confession, belief, and baptism into Him make us recipients and partakers of. The scriptures tell us that life and death are in the power of the tongue (Proverbs 18:22). You cannot be both justified and condemned at the same time.

217

Justification is the response to your condemnation, thus you are condemned no more. It concerns me when I hear believers calling themselves "sinners." Sometimes it is dressed up as, "I'm just a sinner saved by grace." No ma'am! No sir! You are not a sinner any longer. To say you are a sinner is to run back into the courtroom after Jesus stood in for you and yell to the judge, "WAIT, I'M GUILTY!"

John 9:31 says the God doesn't listen to sinners. Romans 5 said, "while we **were** sinners..." You are no longer a sinner. You are a saint.

Part of the war to accept that as your truth is in your consideration of your daily struggles.

> *Romans 3:23*
> *For all have sinned and fall short of the glory of God.*

I am aware that you and I both still have a sin nature in the flesh. To be a sinner means you are in relationship with sin. To be a sinner means you make conscious, consistent decisions to continue in the life of sin, thus reinstating the law of sin and death. To identify yourself as a sinner because of the works of your weakness is to reject the justification of Christ. If justification isn't by works, you cannot undo it by works either. Justification is received by your acceptance and submission to the things of God. You don't cease to be a saint because you slip. You cease to be a saint when you make a conscious decision to believe the truth of your past rather than the truth of the cross. You cease to be a saint when you divorce yourself from the justification of Christ by returning to your own resume. Don't allow another person to call you a sinner. You *were* (past tense) a sinner. But that person no longer lives. It is Christ that lives.

Regeneration is the new birth process. It is a translation of "palingenesia", which means to birth again.

> *I have been crucified with Christ and I no longer live, but Christ lives in me. The life I now live in the body, I live by faith in the Son of God, who loved me and gave himself for me.*
>
> *- Galatians 2:20*

You must make the choice to choose to live as Christ. To be born again as Him. The benefit of regeneration is justification. We've all seen movies where criminals are put in witness protection, right? The first thing they do is give them a new identity, a new record, and new credentials. They move them to a new place, but they have to divorce their old life. The person they were has to completely die so that their new identity can live. The greatest threat to their life as the new person is being identified as the old person. I can imagine that it's hard to have lived your entire life introducing yourself in the way that your parents named you but now you have to come into harmony with a completely new identity. If you introduce yourself as who you were, instantly all of your past enemies, all of your past debts, and all of your past judgments are placed on you again. They can easily find you because you have identified with who you were.

This is how the life of the believer is. At the point where you accept Christ by faith you are placed into witness protection. I like to call it Kingdom asylum. A news blast goes out that you are dead, but the enemy of your past continues looking for any sign that you are still alive. Every time the old you shows up, an attack is launched. The old you can show up in your way of thinking, relating, or living. The old you finds it hard to believe that people can genuinely love you.

The Christ-you believes that you are loved but that many have yet to realize how much they love you. When you begin to relate to people through the mind of the old you, Satan the accuser tries to reinstate charges against you. The old you lives in fear of rejection. The Christ-you looks for affirmation from heaven down. You look to please the Father and are unbothered by a lack of proper perception from peers in the earth. But when you begin to relate to rejection the way the old you did, the accuser locates you and tries to summon a jury against you. In a court of law the jury is always made up of your peers. The enemy will summon a jury of the peers of your past. People who knew you before you knew Christ will tell you, "You'll always be just XYZ to me." Those who know your flaws will be a part of that jury and will always try to remind you of what you were, how you failed, and how you messed up. With a jury like that, condemnation is going to be the guaranteed

judgment.

> *Wherefore seeing we also are compassed*
> *about with so great a cloud of witnesses, let*
> *us lay aside every weight, and the sin which*
> *doth so easily beset us, and let us run with*
> *patience the race that is set before us 2*
> *Looking unto Jesus*
>
> *the author and finisher of our faith; who for*
> *the joy that was set before him endured the*
> *cross, despising the shame, and is set*
> *down at the right hand of the throne of God.*
>
> *_ Hebrews 12:1–2*

When you maintain your standing in Christ, your

peers change. As one of the justified your peers are

the "great cloud of witnesses." Those who knew you

and have not themselves become at one with Christ

no longer qualify to be in your jury. Their bias

disqualifies them from having an opportunity to testify

against you. You are included amongst Abraham, Isaac, and Jacob. It is with this in mind that you have to daily throw off the things that try to pull you back into your old nature. You have to interrupt the patterns and habits that easily entangle you and throw you off of the pathway to sanctification.

Regeneration and justification can be difficult to understand. Even the great religious leader Nicodemus struggled to fully understand this supernatural phenomenon. In John 3 he asked how it was possible. The natural mind will struggle to conceptualize the mystery of the work of regeneration and justification in your life. Jesus' response is that it cannot be explained because it is a work of the spirit. He says in vs. 8 that it's as difficult to explain as it is to tell where wind comes from and where it goes. When you are born again, the direction of thought changes.

You don't think about your spiritual relationship with God from the mind of the flesh. You consider your flesh from the mind of the spirit. You consider your reality from the mind of the spirit. The carnal mind will never understand what it truly means to be born again. You can't start from a carnal paradigm and end in a spiritual revelation. Being born again is a miracle. You are a new creation. That means you are now of the God kind. You are in the family of God. This new family lives by a higher standard of righteousness.

The righteousness of God is not defined by the righteousness of man. When you are truly born again, you even see your human goodness independent of Christ as not being good at all. We are made righteous not of ourselves, but righteousness is imputed to us. God's righteousness is given to us. This means His righteousness is placed on us. Man's standard of righteousness functions from a very base way of thinking. It's right to repay evil for evil to the carnal mind. If someone doesn't like you, to the carnal mind it's right not to like them. But the righteousness of God doesn't work like that.

In God's Kingdom we bless those that curse us. We speak well of those that speak against us.

It's easy to afford someone else justification that they don't deserve when you've truly accepted, embraced, and enjoyed the justification you didn't deserve. When you realize that He has forgiven the past version of you and justified the new you, you easily forgive those who live as you once lived. The justification of the new man is an acquittal. We all need justification because all of us were guilty. We are justified by grace through faith in the work of Christ. Sanctification is the fruit of the person who has embraced justification.

Sanctification means to set apart. Our actions change

because we are sanctified. No! We are not better than anyone else. Our minds, bodies, and souls are just set apart for the use of God. We don't lend them to the use of impure soul ties, conversations of gossip, or ungodly lifestyles. Sanctification is an ongoing process. The more as one we become with Christ the more we commit ourselves to sanctification. Our decisions begin to change. The things we like, love, and find funny change. Righteousness is then judged from heaven down and not Earth up.

I want you to access your relationship to yourself. Do you consider yourself a sinner? Do you still consider yourself as worthless, dirty, and "a worm"? You have to change how you relate to your [new] self. Those things are the truth of your past; they're true of a person that no longer exists. Stop resurrecting the old man and crucifying the new man; it is the old you that must be crucified. The new you must live in, through

and as Christ. Embrace your new you! Your true you!

Chapter Ten

Developing a Kingdom Culture

In order to fully embrace inexhaustible grace you must accept the double-edged sword that it is. The grace of Christ is a benefit of accepting Christ as your Lord and Savior. Though many have accepted Christ as Savior few have accepted Him as Lord. The Lordship of Christ requires an adjustment in the life of the believer. Kingdom citizenship requires defection from the government of the flesh. Defection is giving up allegiance to one state or nation in order to pledge allegiance to another. In order to claim Kingdom citizenship you have to declare independence from the state of being self-willed. You must defect from those ways of thinking, believing, and reacting that seem to come naturally to you. So often we want to take advantage of the benefits of being Kingdom citizens without taking on the responsibilities that come along with it, responsibilities that in and of themselves reflect one's allegiance to the Kingdom of

God and the Lordship of Jesus Christ. Though salvation is not attained by works it is revealed by works.

> *21 Jesus said unto him, If thou wilt be perfect, go and sell that thou hast, and give to the poor, and thou shalt have treasure in heaven: and come and follow me.22 But when the young man heard that saying, he went away sorrowful: for he had great possessions.23 Then said Jesus unto his disciples, Verily I say unto you, That a rich man shall hardly enter into the kingdom of heaven.24 And again I say unto you, It is easier for a camel to go through the eye of a needle, than for a rich man to enter into the kingdom of God. — Matthew 19:16-24*

Matthew 19 contains what I believe to be one of the most misunderstood texts and most misunderstood commands. A young man desperately wants to secure his place in the Kingdom. When Jesus finally tells Him the price for his citizenship, the young man is discouraged. On the surface of the above passage of scripture it would seem to suggest that Jesus has a problem with material prosperity. Many have used this scripture to advocate, justify, and encourage poverty. On the contrary, Jesus has no issue with prosperity. He tells this man what to do with his material possessions. I'd like to ask you a question. Assuming that you confess Christianity I will equally assume that you believe that Jesus has saved you from hell. But can Jesus tell you what to do? Deeper than that, do you (and would you) obey Jesus' instructions? Jesus tells this man the price for his citizenship is transference of ownership. He must give control of all of "his" possessions to the will of the Lord.

As Kingdom citizens we have access to all that the Kingdom has. We simply do not have ownership. The economic system of a kingdom is very different than that of a democracy. The economic system of a kingdom is called a common wealth. The wealth is common. Everyone has access; however, only one has ownership and that's the king.

If you're like the young man you'll hear that as something discouraging. After all, you worked for everything you have, right? Remember when you were a child? You lived life carefree. Your parents were responsible for everything, and if you had good parents they demanded that you not concern yourself with the burden of the household responsibilities. At the same time, you could go and ask them for money for your allowance, money for field trips, and money for games. They provided your clothes, your shoes, your food, and for all of your needs and many of your wants. You were worry-free but had access to the wealth of the house. That's how a common wealth functions. You have all of the access with none of the burden of responsibility.

Remember Matthew 11:29? Jesus said to take His yoke because it was easy and light. It amazes me when I see so many people fight for their burdens and their right to have burdens. Doesn't that sound crazy? "Hey, I want my right to have burdens and carry heavy loads." Not just financial and material responsibilities and possessions but emotional and mental ones too. Kingdom citizens do not claim ownership. As the Lord's people we are entrusted as stewards. The more faithful we are in managing what the Lord has entrusted to our care the more he gives us to care for. The most dangerous thing a manager can do, though, is mistake their role for the role of the owners. They'll attempt to tell the owner when, where, how, and why and end up getting fired for insubordination.

The liberty that comes with being the Lord's people only truly comes when you give everything over to

God. There's a freedom that comes in allowing Him to make the decisions and to be the voice of guidance. The fruit of the tree of Kingdom citizenship is transference of independent power. You give it all to God! As great as America is, the great "American dream" is a trap. The dream of owning the house and the white picket fence. They forgot to tell you about the debt, the burden, the worry, and stress that come along with being the owner. You can live stress-free as Kingdom citizens because you are not principally responsible. The money is in your bank account, but He is responsible for it. The decisions will affect your life, but He is responsible for it. That means, however, that He must have the final say-so. No decision can be made independent of His mind and will if He is going to be responsible for it.

What do you own? What pains, hurts, grudges, and disappointments are burdening you because you own

them? They did it "to you". "Your life" has been
effected by it. Nobody understands because it's "your
life." Those are confessions of a person who has not
defected to the Kingdom of God. Kingdom citizens
don't own anything including the offenses of their
past. Everything we've accrued we give over to
Jesus. You can't receive justification yet want to hold
on to the offenses and grudges of your past. That
person is dead so all of his debts are dead too, not
only the debts he owed but also the things that were
owed to him.

In a previous chapter we looked at Matthew 18:21–29
and the parable about the man who owed someone a
lot of money. The Bible says the debtor decided to
forgive the debt. Then the one who had just been
forgiven went to look for a person who owed him but a
fraction of what he had owed. The Bible says that

man was delivered to tormentors. Do you realize that when you hold grudges (debts) against people, it is you that is tormented? You awaken the old man by claiming the things that are owed to the old man. Justification is again a two-edged sword. Your debts are cancelled, but you too must cancel your rights as a debtor.

The final test of Kingdom Citizenship is your ability to obey the Lord. Can Jesus tell you what to do with "your stuff"? If you take on the mind of "It's my money, my family, my house, my car, my job, my past, my issues," you'll struggle when it comes time to reconcile those things with the Kingdom of God.

I remember one time the Lord told me to sow a large seed into a ministry. I'm a giver so sowing the seed wasn't the problem. The problem was the person that seed would have to go through. The senior leader of that ministry had offended me years before and I didn't want to give him "my money." Then I heard the voice of the Lord correct me; He said, "It's not your money!" Immediately I fell to my knees, prayed and obeyed the Lord.

This is why Jesus said it is more difficult for a rich man to enter the eye of a needle than to enter the Kingdom of Heaven. Matthew 19 has been a topic of conversation amongst many preachers. Some suggest that the "eye of a needle" was a low, narrow entrance into Jerusalem that would require the camel to be stripped of anything it was carrying in order to get through the gates. However, the soundest explanation is that Jesus was employing hyperbole. He was exaggerating so that it could be understood that it's impossible to be saved carrying and owning your own stuff. He has no problem with you prospering but that "your" prosperity must go into the common wealth account. It must become a tool at the disposal of the Kingdom of God. Not only must your things be at His disposal, but you must be at His disposal.

> **The earth is the Lord's the fullness thereof, all the world and they that dwell therein - Psalms 24:1**

We dwell within the earth. That means we belong to God. The more we yield to Him as our King the more of His favor we release to flow in our life. No, it's not that we can earn the favor of God, but we can block it. A life that is not yielded to the will of Christ as King is a life that interrupts the flow of favor into your life. Have you made your life HIS vessel? Have you made your life into HIS tool? Have you made your life His?

The idea of holiness is a frightening one for the average person. Can you really be holy? What is holiness? In its simplest definition holiness means to be set apart. Imagine going to a BBQ and the food is so good that you want to take some home. You prepare a to-go plate, you wrap it up and set it aside. That plate is now "holy". It is "consecrated". It's set aside for a specific use. It is not available to be sampled, tested, tasted, or shared. It is set aside for the owner of the plate. It would be offensive for anyone to come along and eat from that plate when obviously it has been set aside [consecrated/holy] for a specific person. That's how God desires that we live in relationship with Him. Our lives must be like that plate. Set aside at the disposal of the owner. The true work of grace only has the liberty to work in the life of those that live their lives as "holiness unto the Lord."

1 Peter 1:15-16
But as he which hath called you is holy, so be ye holy in all manner of conversation;Because it is written, be ye holy for I am holy.

But wait! Erase that vain, religious, works-driven perception of holiness. Not wearing this, not eating that, not going there. Don't focus on that; experience "holiness" as exclusive dedication. One of the most visible representations of holiness that we have is the marriage covenant between one man and one woman. Their lives are lived through the lens of their commitment and responsibility to the other person. In a healthy marriage you consider how your daily actions will affect your spouse. You opt out of doing certain things, not because of the thing itself but perhaps because of how your spouse feels about it or perhaps because it would take time away from your quality time with your spouse. You make decisions with the consideration of that covenant responsibility in mind. That is how you should relate to holiness.

Don't be intimidated by some religious approach to it. Don't approach it from the lists of "cannots."

Approach it from the lens of commitment to the Lord. It's easy to approach holiness in this way when you take on a Kingdom paradigm. "I belong to the Lord," like that husband or wife that belongs to their spouse, no, not in a dictatorial, unhealthy kind of way but in a loving, freely given, freely received way. That's the commitment the Lord desires from you. As you increase in your degree of commitment to the Lord those things that might have been a part of your way of living and being begin to fall away. They fall away simply because your commitment to the Lord becomes your first priority, not what you want or what makes you happy.

Again, if we look into the marital relationship this is how a healthy covenant should look. The wife gives up her role as her own personal care agent tasked with looking out for herself, pleasing herself, and putting herself first. She gives that role up and gives it over to her husband. The husband in like manner gives up that role in his life and gives it over to his wife. Now they have each become the personal care agent for the other spouse. When you trust the covenant and you trust your spouse's commitment to the covenant, you release that responsibility to them. When you truly trust your covenant relationship with the Lord, you also trust that He commits Himself to your care and pleasure. Commit yourselves to His. With that paradigm in mind, let's look at Matthew 6:25–34 again.

> *25 Therefore I say unto you, Take no thought for your life, what ye shall eat, or what ye shall drink; nor yet for your body, what ye shall put on. Is not the life more than meat, and the body than raiment?26 Behold the fowls of the air: for they sow not, neither do they reap, nor gather into barns; yet your heavenly Father feedeth them. Are ye not much better than they?*

27 Which of you by taking thought can add one cubit unto his stature? 28 And why take ye thought for raiment? Consider the lilies of the field, how they grow; they toil not, neither do they spin: 29 And yet I say unto you, That even Solomon in all his glory was not arrayed like one of these.30 Wherefore, if God so clothe the grass of the field, which to day is, and to morrow is cast into the oven, shall he not much more clothe you, O ye of little faith? 31 Therefore take no thought, saying, What shall we eat? or, What shall we drink? or, Wherewithal shall we be clothed? 32 (For after all these things do the Gentiles seek:) for your heavenly Father knoweth that ye have need of all these things. 33 But seek ye first the kingdom of God, and his righteousness; and all these things shall be added unto you.34 Take therefore no thought for the morrow: for the morrow shall take thought for the things of itself. Sufficient unto the day is the evil thereof.

He says don't worry about things for yourself, He's got that covered! Instead seek ye first His Kingdom and His righteousness. This is the serenity that true grace brings you. I've heard a perverted message of grace that only teaches part of the truth. It teaches God's responsibility to you but leaves out your responsibility to God. Yes, God wants to cover you, cleanse you, and provide salvation to you, but you have a part too. Your part is to lay down your pride and fall into the vulnerability of trust, the trust that makes you vulnerable to being dropped but that's confident that you won't be and still yet more confident that, if you are, you'll run into destiny while lying on the ground, while on your knees dusting yourself off, and while you stand up again.

The Gospel of the Kingdom is the only gospel that Jesus preached. Jesus did not preach the cross. The cross was His demonstration of Kingdom power.

We've spent more time focusing on the demonstration

(the what), but we've lost focus on the lessons (the

why).

> **Luke 9:23**
> **And He said to them all, if any man will**
> **come after me, let him deny himself, and**
> **take up his cross daily, and follow me.**

Have you taken up your cross? Do you take it up

daily? If the answer to either of those questions is

"No," then perhaps the reason is that you don't yet

understand the basic premise of the gospel of the

Kingdom—the message that God is intent on

maintaining dominion in the earth but since God is a

spirit, and the earth is man's, His dominion must then

be administrated through a [hu]man. No, He is not

looking for puppets. He's looking for partners,

partners who can see the bigger picture and submit

their own pursuits to His pursuit. If I submit my plan to His plan and my plan is within His will, then when His plan succeeds, my plan automatically does too.

Psalm 37:5 told us to commit our ways to the Lord, trust Him, and He will bring it to pass. See, taking up your cross, laying down your own will to pick up His, is not a loss. No, quite the contrary, it's a gain. You gain the support of heaven, the backing of the God of the universe, and the assistance of legions of angels. You just went from an individual mom-and-pop operation to a storefront of a major enterprise. Now what took you 12 months to do is done in 12 hours because you've got the equipment of the big enterprise. Grace is that equipment. In order to walk in grace you don't have to cease to be you. God doesn't require that you forfeit your uniqueness, your individuality, and He's not looking for you to be uniformed. You don't have to look like everyone else or do it the same way. He simply desires you to be unified—unified in commitment to His plan, His purpose, and His way. He simply expects that you will become more unified in a truer expression of your divine self. Not the version of you that has been shaped by pains, failures, and synthetic thinking but the version of you that predates your birthdate; the original blueprint version of you that He designed before you were formed in your mother's womb.

I often share with people that an inability to fully submit to the things of God is not a "church" issue, it's a trust issue. The more you trust God the easier it is to let Him do the directing, the guiding, and the shot-calling. He does not desire to be in the driver's seat in your life. He is not the pilot. You are! But a wise pilot listens to the voice of air traffic control. After all, your eyes can only see but so far, but His eyes are in every place (Proverbs 15:3). The voice of the Lord must be the air traffic control in the flight of your life.

What if all of this grace talk doesn't work? What if it's all just talk? Well, I've not written about concepts and revelations that I've simply read, heard, and received. This book's evidence is found in my life and in the life of so many other believers who have truly tapped into God's grace. God's grace is freely given to you, but you must receive it. You must voluntarily yield yourself to its work and administration in your life. The grace of Christ is the new management in your life. When a company changes ownership, it often changes management. New management brings in new principles, new procedures, and a new culture. I believe by faith that as you've read this book you've been coming to the table of conversation and conversion within yourself. The work of grace is not a merger. The work of grace can only be accomplished if it is given total control. Allow God's grace to take over your life.

If by some chance it's all a farce, and I and so many others who live by faith in the grace of Christ just have really good luck, you can always go back to living however it was that you lived before grace. But I promise you; a life truly yielded to grace will find too much comfort in the benefits to ever go back to how life was before. Grace makes heavy work light. It makes daunting things seem small. Grace is a place of refuge, and your submission to grace is never without reward. It grants you access to the Lord's rest, His strength, and His inexhaustible supply.

1 Corinthians 15:55

Death is swallowed up in victory. O death, where is your victory? O grave, where is

your sting? The sting of death is sin, the

power of sin is the law. But thanks be to

God, who gives us the victory through the

Lord Jesus Christ. Therefore my beloved

brothers be steadfast, immovable, always

abounding in the work of the Lord, knowing

that in the Lord your labor is not in vain."

Made in the USA
Columbia, SC
18 May 2020